Delight

to be a Woman of God

Mikaela Vincent

Visit

www.MoreThanAConquerorBooks.com

for more books that make a difference in the lives of those you care about. Follow Mikaela Vincent and
More than a Conqueror Books on

Twitter, Facebook, and Wordpress.

Text and illustrations copyright © 2016 by Mikaela Vincent

More Than A Conqueror Books
MoreThanAConquerorBooks@gmail.com
www.MoreThanAConquerorBooks.com

All Scripture quotations, unless otherwise indicated, are taken from the Holy Bible, New King James Version. Copyright © 1982 by Thomas Nelson, Inc. Used by permission. All rights reserved.
Scripture quotations marked (NIV) are taken from the Holy Bible, New International Version®, NIV®. Copyright © 1973, 1978, 1984 by Biblica, Inc.™ Used by permission of Zondervan. All rights reserved worldwide. www.zondervan.com

Scripture quotations marked (NIV) are taken from the Holy Bible, New International Version®, NIV®. Copyright © 1973, 1978, 1984, 2011 by Biblica, Inc.™ Used by permission of Zondervan. All rights reserved worldwide. www.zondervan.com The "NIV" and "New International Version" are trademarks registered in the United States Patent and Trademark Office by Biblica, Inc.™

Table of Contents

Part 1
Delight in divine relationship

1. Delight in belonging — 10
2. Delight in hunger for God — 12
3. Delight in your betrothal — 14
4. Delight in your King — 16
5. Delight in your beauty — 18
6. Delight in your Father — 20
7. Delight in your inheritance — 22
8. Delight in the Word — 24
9. Delight in worship — 26
10. Delight in experiencing God — 28
11. Delight in the Secret Place — 30
12. Delight in conversing with your King — 32
13. Delight in knowing God's voice — 34
14. Delight in listening to God — 36
15. Delight in following His lead — 38

Part 2
Delight in freedom, joy, and abundant Life

16. Delight in your Counselor — 42
17. Delight in the Truth — 44
18. Delight in freedom — 46
19. Delight in breaking ancient chains — 48
20. Delight in blessing — 50
21. Delight in your Savior — 52
22. Delight in your way out — 54
23. Delight in your focus — 56
24. Delight in surrender — 58
25. Delight in faith — 60
26. Delight in victory — 62
27. Delight in the Spirit — 64
28. Delight in higher heights — 66
29. Delight in deeper depths — 68

Part 3
Delighting in heavenly love for earthly relationships

30. Delight in loving — 72
31. Delight in love's Source — 74
32. Delight in abiding in Love — 76
33. Delight in truthfulness — 78
34. Delight in faithfulness — 80
35. Delight in understanding — 82
36. Delight in forgiveness — 84
37. Delight in your King's Choice — 86
38. Delight in true love — 88
39. Delght in your Healer — 90
40. Delight in freedom and purity — 92
41. Delight in turning the battle around — 94
42. Delight in Kingdom Culture dating — 96
43. Delight in Glorifying God — 98

Leader's Guide for Group Study — 100

Also by Mikaela Vincent:

Delight to Be a Woman of God Prayer Journal
Companion to this book

Dare to Become a Kingdom Culture Leader
Volume 1: One Passion, One Purpose, One King
Volume 2: Oneness and the Watchman Warrior

Dare to Be a Man of God

Dare to Be a Man of God Prayer Journal

Chronicles of the Kingdom of Light
Book 1: Rescue from the Kingdom of Darkness
Book 2: Sands of Surrender

Step into the adventure...

Mikaela Vincent
More Than A Conqueror Books

We're not just about books. We're about books that make a difference in the lives of those you care about.

www.MoreThanAConquerorBooks.com

Deepen your delight, with the

Delight to Be a Woman of God Prayer Journal

companion to this workbook.

Mikaela Vincent

*Packed with tips and guides for learning how to hear God's voice and walk in the Spirit, this prayer journal companion to **Delight to Be a Woman of God** comes with or without lines, so you can write out your prayers to God and His answers. Order now at www.MoreThanAConquerorBooks.com.*

(Author's proceeds go to shining the light of Christ where it's never been before. For more information, write MoreThanAConquerorBooks@gmail.com.)

*To my precious daughter
who delights in her King's love
and so freely pours it out
on everyone around her.*

*And to all my spiritual daughters
who have joined me on this journey
to draw near to our
King of Kings.*

*I cherish every moment
we've laughed together
and danced with Him,
as He dropped down pieces of heaven
and left us in awe of Him.*

*May He bedazzle you
with His beauty
and overwhelm you
with His love
every moment
the rest of your lives.*

Be free!

Suggestions for how to use this devotional:

† **Keep a journal**, such as the *Delight to Be a Woman of God Prayer Journal* companion to this book, available at www.MoreThanAConquerorBooks.com. Choose with or without lines (for those who like to draw and do other creative journaling). This journal is loaded with tips for listening to God's voice and walking as one with Him through life's trials, but really, any notebook will do. You were created for relationship. So think of your journal as letters written by you to the One you love, and from Him to you. Let Him change the way you see things. And keep looking back at what He's teaching you so you won't forget it, and so you can walk out in those truths. *Let Him change your LIFE!*

† **Look up the scriptures in each chapter.** My words don't matter so much. It's His Word that will change you. I like to write in the margins of my Bible the things He is teaching me from each passage. Then, every time I open my Bible to that passage, I'm reminded of His words, and it makes it easier to walk out in that truth.

† **Take your time through each chapter.** Don't be in a hurry to get through this book. Every chapter has deep jewels God wants you to truly learn and walk out in, not just skim through. The daily applications at the end of each chapter are lifestyle-changing, if you let them become a habit rather than something you do just once.

† **Have a daily quiet time.** Don't let a day go by without this important time alone with Jesus. Choose a time in the day that is good for you. Everyone's quiet time is different, so don't feel like yours has to look like someone else's or happen at the same time of day as theirs. Feel free to be creative. I like to start my morning with Jesus, just doing whatever He's doing that day: I worship, listen to Him, pray, read the Word, let Him show me things in my heart He wants to change, or study through a devotional. Then at night, I read through the Bible, so that what He says is the last thing in my mind as I fall asleep.

† **Get your friends involved.** Introduce this devotional to others who will journey with you through it, doing the chapters together with you, or in their own quiet times. You will learn more if you are sharing what you're learning, and hearing what He's teaching others. You might even want to gather together a group to do this as a weekly Bible study. (See suggestions at the end of the book for how to lead a group Bible study.) But if you're still at home, your favorite way to study this book might be together with your mother. After all, God wants her to be a woman of God, too.

You Were Made for Worship

You were made for worship.
You were made for this.
You were made to know the King
so many others miss.
You were made to love Him,
Enjoy Him, feel His touch,
Experience His presence.
Yes, you were made for such.

You were made for mysteries
This world has never known,
To step behind the veil and touch
The foot of High King's throne.
Your knees were made to bow before
The Lover of your soul.
Your hands were made to reach for Him
So He can make you whole.

Don't miss what you were made for.
Don't miss the sweetest bliss
Of life lived out of passion,
Empowered by Jesus' kiss.
For through His love you'll conquer
Every circumstance,
Waltzing in the arms of
This sweet, divine romance.

Part 1:
Delight in Divine Relationship

Delight in belonging

Home is where the heart is

Have you ever felt misunderstood? Out of place? Not accepted? Like you don't belong, especially with certain people? Explain.

_____
_____
_____

You're not alone. Everyone has felt that way at some time in life. Even in the same country or city, what is expected of you in one place is frowned on in another. You could wear yourself out trying to dance to everyone's tune.

Have you ever compromised—done something just to fit in, even though it didn't feel right? How did that work out for you? _____
_____
_____

Friends come and go, and people who want you to do what you know is wrong aren't really friends. *They are not your home.*

If you've given your heart to the King of Kings, then your culture is not of this world; it is *Kingdom Culture*. You are a stranger here, and you will never fit in fully, because *Heaven is now your home.* 1 Peter 1:17; 2:11-12.

Read Jesus' prayer in John 17:13-19. What does it mean to be in the world but not of the world?
_____
_____
_____

What is the world's attitude toward us? Why? What did Jesus give us in verse 14 that sets us apart from the world? _____
_____

Others get their identity from what people think about them or what job they do, but *your identity is in what your King has done for you.* You are *set apart.* Hebrews 10:14, 1 Peter 1:16.

You do things the way your King does, not the way everyone around you wants you to.

I grew up in several countries, so that can make social acceptance a bit awkward. If cultures were colors, whenever I was in the red one, I thought I must be blue; but whenever I was in the blue one, I thought red must be my home.

The truth is I will never be either red or blue. *Life had colored me purple.* And now that I've lived all over the world, that home mix would be even muddier ... but for *Jesus*.

There is a place where you are always accepted, always understood, always loved—Someone who speaks the language of your heart and always wants to hang out with you.

Nothing you do ever shocks Him.

He doesn't make fun of you or put you down.

He will never ask you to do something you shouldn't.

He cherishes everything about you.

He is *captivated by your beauty.*

He will never leave you or forsake you.

He fights for you.

No matter how rocky life gets, He'll never let you down. Hebrews 13:5.

One touch, and He heals you. One moment of truth, and you'll never be the same again. Step into His never-ending love, and you'll be ruined for other loves the rest of your life.

❧ *Jesus is your true Home.*

No matter how different others think you are, you are no surprise to God. He is the One who placed you in the home and culture you grew up in, painted you all those beautiful colors, and knows you better than you know yourself.

Read Psalm 139 and Matthew 10:28-31. How well does God know you, understand you and love you? Explain. _____

What is God's name in Genesis 16:13? _____

Why do you think Hagar called Him that? _____

What are some things about you that only God knows? _____

Your King loves you more than anyone in this world, and knows you better than you know yourself. He has a future planned out for you and it is good—a future with *Himself*. Jeremiah 29:11-14.

Read John 14:23. Where does Jesus call home? _____

> *You are Jesus' home.*

I don't know about you, but I want my heart—the temple of the One I love—to be that place where He leans back, props up His feet and says, "Ah! Mikaela's heart! Now *THIS* is a place I feel at home!" Ezekial 43:7a.

Read Matthew 6:19-21. How could making Jesus your one true Treasure be to your advantage? See 2 Corinthians 4:7-18. _____

Write a letter to your King, asking Him to make Himself at home in your heart, and to help you feel at home with Him.
_____
_____
_____
_____
_____
_____

In what ways have you been walking in worldly culture instead of Kingdom Culture? Ask the Lord and write what comes to mind.
_____
_____
_____
_____

Your heart, His home

Be still before the Lord, close your eyes, and ask Him to show you a picture of His home, your heart. What does it look like? Where are His favorite places to hang out with you? Ask Him. Are there some corners that have been a bit cluttered? Don't try to clean them out on your own. Ask Him to help you.

Delight in hunger for God

Bountiful banquet

What are your favorite foods? Why?

Eating can be a lot of fun. But if you don't eat, what will happen to you?

What if you eat, but not enough or not the right foods? What will happen then?

How does that compare to your spiritual life?

What theme do these verses have in common: Psalm 34:8, 10; Psalm 119:103; and 1 Peter 2:2-3?

What do Isaiah 55:1-2 and John 6:26-27 say?

What claim did Jesus make in John 6:35?

So here's the question: *How hungry are you for God?* Do you go for days without "eating," without reading the Word or having a quiet time? Are you a spiritual baby, only eating when someone else "feeds" you, like at church? Explain.

The problem with ignoring your hunger is eventually it goes away. You could find your spiritual life dying before you realize it.

Read Isaiah 55:6 and Psalm 32:6. When is the right time to seek the Lord?

Jesus is pursuing you right now. He wants to draw you into deeper depths with Him. *Don't miss the moment.* Song of Songs 5:2-6.

School, work, friends, entertainment, a boyfriend, clothes, even youth groups and church aren't enough to satisfy.

You were made for more. **You were made to walk in intimacy with the One who loves you so much He died so you could be His.** *He is the only One Who will truly satisfy your deepest longings.*

Have you ever met someone so close to God that pieces of His character shone through her (him) in ways you longed for too? Explain.

When I see someone walking in depths with the Lord that I don't know yet, experiencing exciting things I long to experience with Him, it makes me *hungry for more.*

It's kind of like watching someone eat your favorite food when you're starving.

I don't know about you, but I want to see miracles, like in the book of Acts. I want dreams and visions, to see God heal the sick and raise the dead. I want to walk so close to Him I hear His voice, smell His fragrance, feel His breath upon my cheek and His arms about me. I want to press my head against His chest and listen to His heartbeat.

It's not enough for me to know Him like I do.

I want to know Him more.

When I was thirteen, I longed for what I saw in other Christians—a bubbly, uncontainable joy that didn't go away, even in the hard times. *I wanted to shine for Jesus all the time.*

So, I surrendered my life to Him—not as the little girl who walked down the aisle at age six—but as the young woman who had *tasted of Jesus and hungered for the whole measure of His fullness in me.* Ephesians 3:16-19.

Now **His joy overflows in me and never leaves no matter how hard things get, because HE is in me and never leaves.** Hebrews 13:5.

But as I sought to live for Him through high school, college and beyond, I thought, "Well, this is wonderful, but is this all there is?" Something inside me still longed for more.

Then I met Edith. That woman *glowed*. Unmarried and in her forties, she spoke of Jesus as her Lover, her *Husband*.

Her relationship with God was strange to me, but not to God, and certainly not to His Word. Check out Hosea 2:16, 19; Isaiah 62:3-5; Isaiah 54:5. Who is God to us? _____

_____

You see, the normal temperature of His bride, the church, is supposed to be *hot*. Lukewarm doesn't cut it. And yet,

The average temperature of God's people today runs so cold that anyone passionate for Him is *accused of having a fever!*

What does Revelation 3:15-16 say?

_____
_____
_____
_____

Scary, isn't it? I don't want to be spewed out of God's mouth, do you?

Well, I must say, Edith's love relationship with God was contagious. I too came to know Him as my Lover and Husband.

This divine love relationship is what we were created for. Ephesians 3:16-19, 1 John 4:19.

Each time I hungered for more of God, He uncovered something in me that needed transformation (Romans 12:2); and as I let Him clean that out and change me, (Hebrews 12:1-3) I could hear His voice louder, feel His touch deeper. *I got more of Him.*

Life is more alive, more abundant, the closer you walk with Jesus. John 10:10.

Colors are more vibrant; the air more fragrant; sunsets more spectacular. Even fun with my friends is all the sweeter.

At any given moment, I can grab hold of His hand, listen to His whisper, and watch Him transform my everyday moments into thrilling, God-awesome ones!

I was blessed to have people in my life who helped me get to deeper depths with the Lord, but if you don't know of anyone like that, the good news is *Jesus is enough*.

You have His Word. You have Him. Now, *dive in*.

It all starts in your quiet times, those moments when you just say "Yes!" to being with Him.

Are you hungry yet? What would you like to experience more of with God? Ask Him for that. Write your prayer here. He wants to spread before you a banquet of His delicious, satisfying love. Song of Songs 2:4.

_____
_____
_____
_____
_____

Make more of Jesus your one desire

*No matter what is around you that feeds your thought life and keeps you busy, **Jesus tastes better**. Psalm 63:1-5. He's spreading before you a banquet of His love, joy, peace and presence. So lay aside all those other crumbs and sit down at the table with the Bread of Life. John 6:33-35.*

Delight in your betrothal

Dove eyes

When I was single, there were times I wondered if I'd ever get married. Not only was I afraid Jesus would come back before I had the chance, but all the Godly men I knew were either taken or not interested. Have you ever felt that way? Explain. _____

_____

Yearning for romance didn't make things easier. I dreamed of a strong, handsome man to sweep me off my feet with whispers of, "How beautiful you are, my love. Your eyes are…"

Yes, I know. Sounds like a movie. But that was my deepest longing. You see,

> *I was made for love, and in loving and being loved I am complete.*

But, alas, the only person who ever told me my eyes were beautiful was my mom.

As different friends paired off and got married, that desire for love and romance drove me to plead with God, "Either bring me the one you have for me or, please, take this yearning away."

He was the right place to go. He'd pour His love over me, satisfy me with His presence, abate my desire ... for a week or two, and then it would all come crashing back in on me again, and there I'd be once more in a heap at His feet asking Him to take the longing away. But each time I went to God, He was faithful to fill me with His love.

Then one day, as I looked around at all the men I knew, I realized *none of them was exciting enough to fill the empty spaces in my heart.*

The One I longed for *had been with me all along!*

God Himself had placed that desire for love in my heart for a purpose, and it wasn't meant to be filled by a man—well, not an earthly one, at least.

What freedom there is in surrender. I soared through a whole year on the wings of Christ's love, never once returning to my place of anguish. **Jesus was more than enough to fill every need.**

And then—

Oh, how I love the "and thens" God tosses into my lap after I surrender to Him.

—My husband appeared! We fell in love, got married, had children, and no, Jesus didn't come first—well, at least not in the way I imagined.

This Godly husband my Heavenly One brought me loves me, fights for me, has eyes only for me, and is the most handsome man alive (in my opinion, of course).

But he is not God.

One day, in my quiet time, I felt Jesus' still, small voice whisper, "Do you want to know how much I love you? Open Song of Songs." As I read, He enclosed me in His strong arms and poured His love over me like a fountain.

Then He spoke to my deepest longing, the one He had placed in me so long ago....

> *"How beautiful you are, my darling!*
> *Oh, how beautiful! Your eyes are doves."*
> Song of Songs 1:15 (NIV)

The King of Kings who loves me *saw* me, empty spaces and all, and *knew* me.

You see, doves have tunnel vision. They focus straight ahead and aren't easily distracted. They also mate for life; like "homing pigeons," they return again and again because they're bound to that one who is their *home*....

With eloquent poetry, my Lover said to me He sees my eyes fixed unwaveringly on Him and my heart bound to His, and calls me *beautiful*.

The world somehow changed for me that

day. When I walked out of my quiet time, either I looked different or something changed in the spiritual realm, because now that my King had declared it, others also began telling me how lovely my eyes are, including my husband, who is not the romantic, quote-poetry-to-his-wife type.

Perhaps my eyes became beautiful when I fixed them on Him and saw myself through *His* eyes.

God delights in answering our deepest desires with Himself.

Was it a set up? Probably. You see, God's love is jealous. He made me for Himself, to walk in the whole measure of the fullness of His love (Ephesians 3:16-19), to know Christ as the fulfillment of my every desire.

"Delight yourself also in the Lord, and He shall give you the desires of your heart." Psalm 37:4

A few years ago, we traveled to Australia just as God was curing me of a terrible, painful, *incurable* disease. I found myself daily in awe of His love, realizing He could do *anything*. **A miracle is a simple thing for Almighty God.**

It wasn't whale season, but I still longed to see one. I didn't quite ask Him for that, though. I think I felt selfish. After all, He was already healing me....

But one morning, I looked past my children's little bodies digging in the sand, and only 200 yards out into the sea breeched the most magnificent whale! He hit the sky so close I could see the ribbing on his chest. I gasped and pointed. Then another breeched. And another. More than a dozen tails slapped the air!

I shouldn't be surprised. *God is like that.*

He loves to display His love in extravagant measures when we look for Him.

But He still thrills me with the surprises of His love. Sometimes every day. And He wants to surprise *you*, too.

You are His bride, made for intimacy with the King of Kings. Isaiah 62:4-5, Revelation 22:17.

If you look for His love every day, He will display it. Quite lavishly, in fact.

What is God's name in 1 John 4:16-18? How does that make you feel? _____
_____
_____

Is Jesus your greatest desire, or is there something you long for more? Explain.
_____
_____
_____

No woman gets everything she wants in this life, unless her desire is for God. Then He most certainly will satisfy her with HIMSELF!

Ask Him to surprise you with His love

Ask God to delight you with His love today in some way that is so straight from His heart to yours that you'll know that was Him. Then walk through your day looking for His love gift.

Delight in your King

Stepping like a princess

When you chose Jesus as your Lord, you became a daughter of the Most High. That makes you a princess. 1 John 3:1.

And as the *bride of the King of Kings* (Revelation 19:6-8), you are destined to be a *queen* and *reign with Him forever.* Revelation 22:5.

How does that make you feel? _____

> **Your King is in love with you.** Song of Songs 4:9.

"Listen, o daughter, consider and give ear: Forget your people and your father's house. The King is enthralled by your beauty; honor him, for He is your Lord." Psalm 45:10-11 (NIV)

Did you hear that? Forget what you used to be, forget what everyone else says you ought to be. *Listen to your King.*

This King of Kings who created the world—who is so magnificent not even the heavens can contain His glory—is captivated by your beauty. **He is head-over-heels in love with you.**

Jesus has prepared a castle for you beyond your wildest dreams, (John 14:1-3) and a feast for your wedding with Him that puts earthly kings to shame. Revelation 19:7-9. He is clothing you in a dazzling, royal robe to wear on that day. Psalm 45:13-14. It's not a fairy tale. It's true. Song of Songs 4:9.

> **Your King dances with you.** Galatians 5:25.

Like your very own Cinderella story, this handsome King (Song of Songs 5:10-16) stole you away from slavery (John 8:34-36) and ashes (Isaiah 61:1-3), and has given you new life as His beloved bride. Isaiah 62:3-5, Ezekial 16:1-14.

So dance! Your life is a ballroom. **Live every moment in the arms of the One who loves you.** Look into His eyes, and let Him take the lead through every situation, as you keep in step with Him. Galatians 5:25; Hebrews 12:2. If you don't know the steps, don't worry. *He does.*

> **Your King fights for you.** Isaiah 42:10-16; Psalm 94:16-19.

Read Song of Songs 3:6-11, and picture Jesus as your King. What is He ready to do for you?
_____
_____
_____

What is His favorite crown? _____

How does that make you feel? _____

This Almighty King who loves you beyond any earthly understanding of love not only fights for you, but He has given the ultimate display of love:

> **Your King gave His life for you.** John 15:13; Romans 5:8.

This Most High over all the heavens and earth stepped into the mortal body of a man so He could die, *just so He could show you how much He loves you.* Philippians 2:6-11.

Although He is holy and blameless, He took upon Himself the punishment that should have been yours, (Isaiah 53:6) breaking the curse of sin and death forever so you could be free. 1 Corinthians 15:55.

Now, *that's* a love worth living for! How do you respond to a love like that?

1 John 4:19: _____
1 John 5:3a: _____
Psalm 45:11: _____
Psalm 95:6: _____

One time, as I was hiking through the mountains in the country where we live, a girl from an isolated village joined me. I shared with her about God's love as we walked along. She replied, "If there's a God who loves me like that, then I want to love Him back!"

Yes. Amen. That's exactly why we love the King: *because He first loved us.* 1 John 4:19.

This King of Kings who calls you to obey Him always has your good in mind because He loves you, even more than you love yourself. Luke 12:7.

That makes me feel safe. It makes me want to obey Him. How about you? How does knowing your King is good affect your fealty to Him?

_____
_____
_____

Is there anything God's asking you to do that you haven't stepped into yet? What's keeping you from obedience?

_____
_____
_____

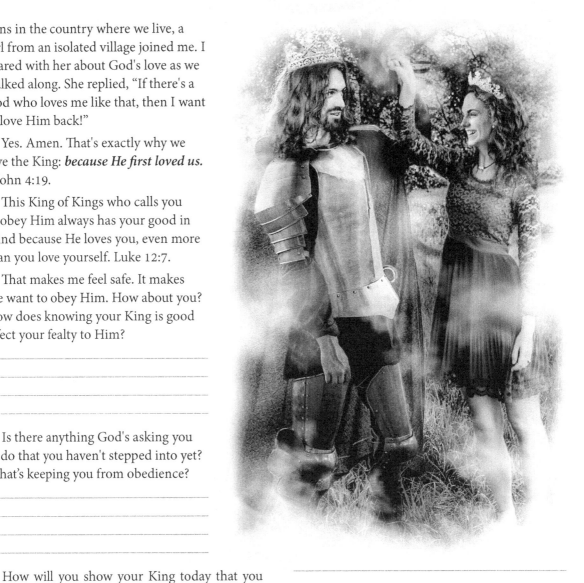

How will you show your King today that you love Him? _____
_____
_____

Take a few moments to bow before the Lord, worship Him and thank Him for the amazing ways He has demonstrated His love for you.

Now pledge Him your love, your life. Write your prayer here. _____
_____
_____

_____
_____
_____
_____
_____

God alone knows what lies ahead. And He is *for* you. If you rely on your own understanding, you could end up on a dangerous road. Proverbs 3:5-6; 16:29. But walking in God's love brings joy and true meaning in this life; not to mention unspeakable treasures in the next.

Falling in love with the King is key to obeying Him. John 14:15. And loving and obeying Him are key to a life filled with joy and freedom. Psalm 119:24, 32.

Delight in your beauty

Mirror, mirror of the Word

"You need to be so beautiful your husband will never look anywhere else," my father advised as I entered my teen years.

But I had a problem. My mother had been a beauty queen, and I sure didn't have what she had. And my friends all seemed to have skin, eyes, hair and curves more pleasing than mine.

I dieted, but that didn't change the size of my hip bones. In fact, the smaller my waist got, the bigger my hips looked. I could spend an hour curling my hair, but the humid climate where we lived sucked the curls straight within minutes.

I told God I wished He'd made my eyes lapis lazuli blue, my skin smooth and white as pearls, and my hair so black it shone violet in the sun. But, alas, I was stuck with yellow skin and freckles.

Is there anything about yourself you wish you could change? _____
_____
_____
_____

God had mercy on me and gave me a husband who fell in love with who I am more than what I look like. In fact, as a newlywed, I'd roll out of bed with my eyes all puffy and my hair all askew; and he'd gaze at me in wonder, whispering, "You're so beautiful!" But when I put on makeup, fixed my hair and wore some dress I thought looked terrific on me, *he wouldn't say anything at all.*

Apparently, his idea of beauty didn't match the world's, or even mine. And I'm *so* glad.

But no matter how sweet my husband is, I still had a problem: Every time I looked in the mirror I saw my flaws; I knew *I didn't measure up.*

In John 8:42-47, Jesus explained that if we listen to the father of lies long enough, his words start feeling true. Then when the One Whose name is Truth speaks, *it sounds like a lie.*

So, as I read that passage in my quiet time one day, it prompted a question: "Is there anything You're saying, Lord, that feels like a lie to me?"

This is the verse He brought to mind:

"All beautiful you are, my darling; there is no flaw in you." Song of Songs 4:7 (NIV)

"You're right," I replied. "I've seen my flaws and know them well. But I want to believe You. Can You show me more Scripture on that?" He did.

Believe this too, beloved creation of the King, and *be free*: You are *perfect*. From your head all the way down to your toes—absolutely, breathtakingly, captivatingly flawless. Song of Songs 4:1-7; 7:1-7. Not because the world says you are, but because *He* says so; for **He has made you so.** Hebrews 10:14.

The One who thought you up in His heart and created you for the purpose of love formed you unique, one of a kind. He dreamed up the color of your hair, your lovely eyes, and the tone of your skin to match. He pieced together your bones, thought up that perfect nose of yours, and shaped your body. Psalm 139:13-14.

There is no one else in this world like you, and never will there be. You are unrepeatable, one of a kind. And **God doesn't make junk, only masterpieces.** In fact, you are made *in His image*. Genesis 1:26-27; Psalm 45:10-13.

"You have stolen my heart, my sister, my bride; you have stolen my heart with one glance of your eyes....
How beautiful you are and how pleasing, o love, with your delights!" Song of Songs 4:9; 7:5-6 (NIV)

That's how God sees you. *Yes, you!* You are gorgeous, delightful, a true heart-throb. Your hair is perfect, your nose is perfect, your eyes are perfect, your waist is perfect… your hips, your thighs, your toes, your chest, your knees, your hands, and who you are inside—all *perfect*. Do you get it?

Don't let what you think the mirror says or what others say tell you any different. You are altogether lovely, and that's that!

Only God's opinion matters. Only what HE says is truth. Believing anything else just isn't worth it. John 8:31-32.

Read Song of Songs 8:8. I know it talks about certain body parts and all, but bear with me. What did the bride's friends think of her? What were they so worried about? _____
_____

Did those friends want to fix her problem? (v 9) How? _____
_____

But she didn't need fixing, after all, did she? Why? How did her betrothed see her? (v 10)
_____
_____

Did she see herself as her friends saw her or as he saw her? (v 10) _____
_____

If you compare yourself to models or movie stars, or let others' opinions skew your viewpoint, you could fall into one of Satan's traps—overeating, low self-esteem, anorexia, plastic surgery....

You need to see yourself through the eyes of the only One whose opinion matters— *your Bridegroom.*

"As the bridegroom rejoices over the bride, so shall your God rejoice over you." Isaiah 62:5b

The root word in Hebrew for bride actually means one who is "perfect" or "complete." *You are made perfect and complete through your betrothal to the King of Kings.*

"For by one sacrifice he has made perfect forever those who are being made holy."
Hebrews 10:14 (NIV)

Perfect on the outside, perfect on the inside—not because you deserve it or because you're all that, but just because *He loves you.*

With your eyes closed, picture Jesus, the Perfect One, standing before you. Now, hand Him all the things you don't like about yourself. Now, ask Him how He sees you. Song of Songs 1-8. Write what you feel Him saying.

_____
_____
_____
_____
_____

True humility is agreeing with God. It's not putting yourself down, like the world thinks it is. That's just another form of pride. **Your eyes are fixed on yourself when you disagree with your King.**

Unless you look down on others, thinking you're better in some way to them, *you are actually walking in humility when you believe you are beautiful.*

In fact, something changes, both within you and in the spiritual realm when you agree with God and walk in His truth.

People who never commented on your beauty before may suddenly shower you with compliments because,

Whenever you believe the truth and walk in it, that truth becomes who you are.

Let the Truth you know be the Truth you live

You are what you believe. Write Song of Songs 4:7 on a card and put it up on the mirror. You want to remember what your King says every time you look at yourself, because His words are the only truth. Anything else you believe is a lie that could take you captive. John 8:42-47, 2 Corinthians 10:3-5. **The only TRUE way to see yourself is in the mirror of the Word.** *James 1:22-25.*

Delight in your Father

My Father, my Daddy

I have this favorite place where I feel safe and protected. All my troubles and worries fade away, and I know that no matter how many things I've done wrong or what anyone else thinks of me, I am loved and delighted in.

It's my Daddy's lap.

I can crawl up into His strong arms, lay my head on his heart, close my eyes, and melt into a sweet sigh of "This is where I belong."

Whatever troubles shot me to His feet in the first place just evaporate in that embrace. I know He'll protect me; and no matter how many mistakes I've made, He loves me and forgives me. Psalm 18; Psalm 91, Psalm 145, Psalm 103, I John 1:9.

You see, my Daddy's love is unconditional. He doesn't love me because I'm perfect or beautiful, even though He says I am. Song of Songs 4:7. *He loves me because I'm his little girl.* 1 John 3:2.

❧ **Your Father loves you.** 1 John 3:1a.

If you have chosen Jesus as your Savior (John 3:16, Romans 10:9), then you are the adopted daughter of the God who loves you.

Prayerfully read 1 Peter 5:7; Isaiah 40:11; Deuteronomy 33:27; Mark 10:13-16; 1 John 4:16; John 14:23; and Psalm 5:11-12. What is the Father like? _____
_____
_____
_____
_____

❧ **He is good.** Nahum 1:7; Psalm 142:7.

Write down some qualities of God's goodness in Psalm 103:1-13. _____
_____
_____

❧ **He cares for you.** Matthew 7:7-11.

What does 1 John 5:14-15 say about your Daddy's love for you? _____
_____
_____

Do you believe that's true? _____

What kind of future does God have prepared for you? See Jeremiah 29:11. _____
_____
_____

God loves you. **He is for you.** Psalm 25. **He fights for you.** Isaiah 42:10-17. **He knows the plans He has for you, and they are good.**

❧ **He picks you up.** Psalm 37:23-24.

When my babies were just learning to walk, their wobbly knees and unsteady feet toppled them to the floor time and again. Their father picked them up, brushed off the dirt, helped them to stand, spread his arms wide, and said, "Come to me. You can do it." They fixed their eyes on their father, and made it!

How is that earthly picture like 1 John 1:9 and Hebrews 12:1-3? _____
_____
_____
_____

God's the One who made you. He knows your every thought. He knows when you're running well, and when you're still a bit wobbly.

Trust His gentle discipline. Hebrews 12:7-13. He has a plan to grow you in every area of your life so you can become the beautiful woman of God He created you to be. Ephesians 4:13.

❧ **He is for you.** Psalm 139:7-10.

My earthly dad isn't perfect by any means. But

he modeled love so well that it's easy for me to run to my Heavenly Father whenever I'm hurting. I know He is always there for me.

But a woman whose earthly father was too busy for her or abandoned her might struggle with the fear that God isn't listening to her prayers, that He's abandoned her too.

God is not like earthly fathers, He is perfect. And His love for you is perfect. What does Deuteronomy 4:31 and 31:8 say? _____
_____

To an abused child, the thought of an all-powerful Heavenly Father could be scary. She might imagine Him as a towering figure holding a stick in His hand, ready to beat her for the slightest mistake. But what do Psalm 86:15 and 1 John 1:9 say about God? _____
_____

The daughter of judgmental or manipulative parents might struggle with the need to earn her Heavenly Father's love, not realizing she already pleases Him just because she's His.

What is your earthly father like? How has that influenced the way you see your Heavenly Father? Do you sometimes find it hard to trust God? Ask Him and write what comes to mind.
_____
_____
_____
_____

What do Psalm 27:10 and Psalm 68:5 say?
_____
_____
_____
_____

Write out a prayer for yourself based on Ephesians 3:16-21. _____
_____
_____
_____
_____
_____
_____
_____

Now picture yourself resting in your Heavenly Father's arms, with your head against His chest, listening to His heart. What does that picture say to you?
_____
_____
_____
_____

Believe what your Father says

Ask God, "What lies do I believe about You that keep me from receiving the fullness of Your love?" Now ask for His truth. What does His Word say about His love for you? Do a Word Search (Chapter 8) and find out.

Delight in your inheritance

Reach beyond the stars

Read 2 Corinthians 4:17-18. What should we fix our eyes on? Why? _____
_____
_____
_____

Soon every trial will end; every wrong done against you will be set right; and sorrow, pain and suffering will disappear. Revelation 7:14-17.

You are a stranger on this earth, just passing through, a sojourner on your way home to heaven. **This is your tiny window of opportunity to prepare for eternity.** *And it's rushing by fast.*

People all around you are trying to get ahead in this life, without thought to what comes next. They want to get married, land a good job, buy a nice car, become famous, make money. But what does Matthew 6:19-21 say?

_____
_____
_____
_____
_____

You, daughter of the King, were created for better things, deeper things, *eternal* things.

Whether or not you get married here on this earth is not as important as how you treat the people God has placed in your life now. What job you get doesn't count as much as shining His light whatever you do. Where you live is nothing compared to **living for Him wherever you are.**

Of course, if God leads you to marry the one He's prepared for you, to take the job He opens the door to, or to live in a particular place, then *your obedience to Him is eternal*, as well. **You won't want to miss the rewards, even here on this earth, of living in the center of His will.**

But I'm urging you to cast aside your longing for earthly things and fix your eyes on eternal ones.

Living like heaven matters changes everything, *even you!*

Weary and longing to rest, my friend Wendy got on a crowded bus. She saw an open seat, but the woman next to it wouldn't let her sit down because she was saving it for someone else. Perturbed, Wendy thought just what she might say to that woman, and it wasn't nice.

Suddenly, Jesus whispered to her heart: "I've saved a seat for you and it is yours forever!" Revelation 3:21.

In that split second, her attitude changed. Rather than lashing out at the lost lady without a seat in heaven, she spent the bus ride praying for her and looking for ways to show her God's love.

Every minute is a new opportunity to be done with sin and move on to the things that matter.

If someone does something against you, you could choose unforgiveness and vengeance, which will only lead your heart into dark, dangerous places. But if you remember heaven and all the blessings that are yours because Christ freely forgave you, it's likely you'll forgive others too.

- **Forgiveness is eternal.** Matthew 6:14; Colossians 3:13.

Hurting people hurt people, after all. You could have compassion on the person who hurt you, ask her what's going on in her life and pray for her. Loving like that builds eternal riches into her life, and yours as well, because ...

- **Love is eternal.** 1 Corinthians 13:8, 13.

But bitterness and unforgiveness won't do you any earthly—or heavenly—good.

An earthly mindset just leads to more pain and bitterness. But a heavenly mindset leads to freedom and joy. 1 Corinthians 2:16; Psalm 119.

This is your opportunity to draw close to the One you love in ways you won't be able to in heaven. In heaven there are no people to wrong you, no battles to fight, no temptation, no sin, no problems to be solved, no trials to go through, no reasons to cry.

You won't need comforting, because there won't be any grief. You won't need your King to ride in on His white horse and rescue you, because you won't fall captive to anything but His glory and majesty. Revelation 7:14-17.

But now, *right now,* while you're here on this earth, surrounded by sin and grime and Satanic forces raging against you, *you can know your Savior in deep, intimate ways that collide heaven with earth*—peace in the midst of the storm, love in the face of hatred, mercy that triumphs over violence, freedom to break every chain....

You see, daughter of the King, **you are in training for reigning.** 2 Timothy 2:11-13; Revelation 22:3-5.

Heaven is open to you—the riches of His love and glory available for you to experience right here, right now, in the midst of brokenness and chaos.

With that in mind, a long line at the grocery store turns into an opportunity to pray for the lost and share Christ; a painful injury becomes a journey of faith; an illness that lands you in bed offers precious time alone with God; angry words spoken in haste become a chance to humbly ask forgiveness, shining God's love and grace even through your mistakes.

Smiling at a clerk who has had a bad day, telling a friend you love her, giving away something precious to you in order to bless someone else, writing a note to say, "Thank you," are all eternal acts, tiny though they may seem.

Each act of love, worship, and obedience piles up riches for you in heaven.

Earthly treasures are of no use in heaven; and even if they were, you can't take them with you. 1 Corinthians 9:24-27; Matthew 6:19-21.

You need everlasting treasures, so when you stand before the King, *you will have something of worth to lay at His feet.* Revelation 2:10; 4:9-11.

"For our light affliction, which is but for a moment, is working for us a far more exceeding and eternal weight of glory, while we do not look at the things which are seen, but at the things which are not seen. For the things which are seen are temporary, but the things which are not seen are eternal."
2 Corinthians 4:17-18

What earthly things occupy your mind right now? School? Work? Guys? TV? Social media? What university to go to? What job to take? Write a prayer to God, handing all those things over to Him. Ask Him to give you a heavenly mindset, so you can see life through His eyes.

_____
_____
_____

Take some time to clean out your heart before the Lord. Then ask Him to open up heaven everywhere you go. What piece of heaven does He want to shower down on you and those you will meet today? Ask Him, and get ready to step into His love and pour it out on others. At the end of the day, write what eternal things you saw and did together with Him.

_____
_____
_____
_____

Eternal mindset—

Don't be so concerned with earthly advantages, but seek the eternal ones that come from loving God and loving others. Matthew 6:19-21; 22:37-40. More important than getting something done is loving the people in your path. More important than finding a husband is loving the Husband you have. Isaiah 61:10. Ask God to open up heaven and spill out the sweetness and power of His presence. Let Him use you to hand out pieces of heaven here on earth to every person you meet, like love, joy, healing, hope, kindness, patience, mercy....

Delight in the Word

Divine dance

What are some of Jesus' names in Revelation 19:11-16? _____
_____
_____

Which descriptions in that passage speak of His power? _____
_____
_____

And what comes out of Jesus' mouth? _____

Which one of Jesus' names in the above passage corresponds with John 1:1, 14? _____

† **The Word is Jesus.** John 1:1, 14.

Wow. That's powerful. Whenever I open up my Bible and read, *I am with the King of Kings, gazing into His eyes, listening to His heart, knowing Him.*

He's not dead. Mohammed, Buddha, and other leaders of worldly religions went to their graves and stayed there. But not Jesus. He rose again. He is alive! 1 Timothy 4:10. **He's with me all the time.**

What does Hebrews 4:12 say about the Word? _____
_____
_____

† **The Word is our sword.** Ephesians 6:17.

We are at odds with a fierce enemy armed to the hilt. He has been waging war for thousands of years. What would happen if you went into battle against such an enemy without a weapon? Isaiah 1:5-6.
_____
_____

Your enemy has plans for you. And if you're not on the alert, fully armed and standing bold against his schemes, you just might fall. Ephesians 6:10-18, I Peter 5:8-9.

It's not enough to read the Word sometimes. We need His Word all the time, because life is constant war. Ephesians 6:10-18; Psalm 51:6.

My most beloved Bible—the one with handwriting and tear stains across the worn pages—fits in the back pocket of my jeans. Whenever I buy a new handbag, I check first to make sure my "sword" fits. That way it's in its "sheath" when I need it.

I love my friend Dini's attitude. When she first came to the Lord, the only Bible she had was a huge, heavy one she carried around in her purse.

Someone asked, "Isn't it hard carrying that thing around all the time?"

"Carrying a cross and dying on it was hard," she laughed. "Carrying around a book about it? Not so much."

† **The Word kisses us.** Song of Songs 1:2.

Write about a time you felt God speaking straight to your heart as you read the Bible.
_____
_____
_____

That was a "kiss" from the God Who loves you. He knows you better than you know yourself. He knows your past and what is yet to come. He knows exactly the word you need for this very moment in your life that will propel you forward to not only make it through, but to *soar*. Deuteronomy 32:11.

So how do you receive a God-kiss? **Open the Word and read it!**

Not long ago I came under attack by friends I love dearly. It was one of the most painful experiences of my life, but it was also one of the most beautiful, because *Jesus danced with me.*

I felt so weak, but His strong arms held me. I didn't know how to respond or what steps to take, but He led the way.

His Word healed me (Psalm 107:19-20) and gave me strength to forgive and speak the truth in love whenever they came at me with false accusations. Romans 12:9-21; Luke 6:37; Ephesians 4:15.

Finally, my attackers said, "Why do you always come out on top?"

Not sure what they meant, I handed their words to the Lord, and then went about my day, resting in Him and knowing He would answer me. That night, as I snuggled under the covers for my "goodnight kiss," this is what the Word said:

"If you pay attention to the commands of the Lord… and carefully follow them, you will always be at the top, never at the bottom."
Deuteronomy 28:13 (NIV)

Now, what do you think it took for God to set up that kiss? For one thing, the way I do my Bible reading at night is I start in Genesis and read to Revelation, a few verses every night so I can focus on each truth and let it sink in deep. That means, *it could take me 2-3 years to read the whole Bible.* **He had to orchestrate that I would be precisely at that passage that very day that my accusers confronted me with that question.**

Now *that's* amazing love!

If I let my King take the lead in my life, His strong arms and His boundless love hold me and keep me from falling, even if I stumble. He whispers into my heart, and I press in closer to Him to keep in step, dancing to the rhythm of His heartbeat of love for me. Galatians 5:25.

† **The Word changes us.** 2 Timothy 3:16-17.

My heart would have fared much differently in the above trial if I had leaned on my own understanding instead of the Lord's. Proverbs 3:5-7.

I had a choice: I could let the blows beat me up, or I could let God use that trial to show me lies and sin in my own heart so His truth could set me free. 2 Corinthians 10:3-5.

He turned my pain into joy (Isaiah 61:3); stilled my fear with His love (1 John 4:18); and gave me grace for my accusers. Matthew 7:1-5; Ephesians 4:2, 26-27.

He also unearthed in me a deep need to be loved by people, and then set me free from the lies that undergirded that stronghold by filling that need with Himself.

You see, *every trial He allows us to face is a chance to draw closer to Him.*

† **The Word sets us free.** John 8:31-32.

Whatever you're going through, you'll find the key to freedom and joy in God's Word.

Why is it important to read the Bible every day?
_____
_____

Did the Word "kiss" you today? How?
_____
_____
_____
_____

Read through the following passages, letting God's love flow into you and fill any empty places: Isaiah 54:10; Isaiah 58:11; Isaiah 41:10, 43:1-2; John 15:7. Write in your journal what He says to you. Then "kiss" Him back: sing to Him, say those scriptures back to Him, write Him a poem or a love letter in your journal, draw Him a picture that says how much you love Him….

Word Search

One great way to combat enemy attacks on your heart is to do a Word Search. Look up in a Bible concordance (there are some online) whatever it is you're struggling with and study the scriptures with those key words in them. For instance, if discouragement is your issue, look up "discourage," "weary," "faint," and also the opposites of "strength," "courage," "might" and "strong." Write in your journal what God shows you, so you can see the pattern of His truth and let Him plant it deep in your heart.

Delight in worship

Living your sacrifice

"But the hour is coming, and now is, when the true worshipers will worship the Father in spirit and truth; for the Father is seeking such to worship Him." John 4:23-24

In the Old Testament, the priests sacrificed animals on the temple altar so God would forgive them of their sins. But was that enough? What does Isaiah 29:13 say? _____
_____

What did God want from His people more than their sacrifices? See Psalm 51:15-17, Psalm 40:6, and 1 Samuel 15:22. _____
_____
_____

Sacrifice was meant to demonstrate how serious sin is—so serious *it deserves death*. When they laid that animal on the altar, God hoped His people would weep over their sins and turn to Him. But it all became a mere ritual, *an act they performed while their hearts were somewhere else.*

Do you ever feel that way? Like your mind and heart are somewhere else when you worship? Explain. _____
_____

God loved us so much He sent His Son as the final, perfect sacrifice. John 3:16. When you invited Jesus to be your Savior, something radical happened in the spiritual realm:

The God who created the heavens and the earth, who is so vast no mind can comprehend Him, so wide no universe can contain Him, came into your tiny, human heart and made it His home. Now, *you are His temple*. 1 Corinthians 3:16.

In other words,

Worship happens inside you before your seat ever hits that church pew.

† **True worship is LIVED.**

It happens as you wake up and hand your day over to the Lord, ... as you sing Him a song on the way to class or work, ... as you praise Him for something wonderful He's done, ... as you go through difficulties and surrender to His will, ... as you help someone in need, ... as you ask the Lord what job to take, ... as you seek God for the husband He has for you, ... as you see a sunset and turn your heart to the One who painted it....

Write Galatians 2:20 in your own words.
_____
_____
_____
_____

Something dies on the altar of the temple of your heart ... *you!*

Read Colossians 3:1-17. What do you die to?
_____
_____
_____
_____

What do you fix your eyes on? (v 1-4)
_____
_____

Does that focus change you? How? (v 12-17)
_____
_____
_____

When you truly fix your eyes on God you can't help but worship Him. Humility is easy to "wear" when you're in the presence of One so much greater than you. You feel the enormity of His unending love, grace and compassion for you, and your anger toward others crumbles.

† **Worshiping God transforms both you and what you're going through.**

Humbly recognizing God as Sovereign and bowing before Him in worship places you in the flow of His leading. Not only will *peace* fill your heart and *serving Him become more important to you than the outcome of your trial*, but He may even give you just the instructions you need to overcome. *Or change the situation altogether.* He is Almighty, after all.

† **Worship is what you were created for.**

Within you is a God-sized hole that can only be filled with knowing your Maker personally, feeling His great love for you, loving Him back, bringing Him glory as you love others through His love, and enjoying Him.

When we worship God, we honor Him for Who He is, and He delights in our praises.

What are some of God's many names in the Word that show He is worthy of worship?

1 Peter 4:19 _____
Deuteronomy 33:27 _____
Jeremiah 16:19 _____
Isaiah 54:5 _____
Genesis 16:13 _____
Exodus 15:26b _____
Other _____

How has God personally demonstrated those aspects of His character to you? _____
_____
_____
_____
_____

Sometimes we can get so preoccupied with how big our problems are *we forget how big our God is.* But when we fix our eyes on Him, our worries shrink in the light of His majesty.

† **Worship is powerful.**

What do these verses say about the power of worship?

Isaiah 30:32: _____

2 Chronicles 20:21-22: _____

Exodus 23:25-27: _____

1 Samuel 16:23: _____

When we worship God, Satan's plans are defeated. He is no match for the Almighty! Not by a long shot. In fact, *Satan himself must bow to the King of Kings.* Philippians 2:10.

† **Worship is a winning strategy against Satan.**

Have you ever had a nightmare or woken up in a panic? Next time that happens,

1. **Tell fear, panic, violence, etc. to flee.**
2. **Worship God.** Sing to Him, put on your favorite praise music, declare His love, mercy and power, or quote a psalm. James 4:7-8.
3. **Use the Galatians 5:22-23 Gauge** in Chapter 16 to work through the memory of that dream with the Lord, so He can set you free and restore your peace.

Worship invites God near and makes Satan flee.

David knew the power of praise as warfare. Psalm 18. Nearly every one of his psalms that begins with how terrible his enemy is ends with how great his God is.

But David loved the Lord too much to just worship whenever he was afraid; *he worshiped God with his life.* Acts 13:22.

Worship is lived

Don't wait until Sunday morning to worship God. Worship Him in your quiet times, and be a living sacrifice to the One you love every moment through your thoughts, words, decisions and the way you live.

Delight in experiencing God
The power of His presence

As my friend and I prayed together in a dingy hotel room in the dark country where we live, we burst into spontaneous praise. Nothing fancy. No piano, no guitar, no hymnal. We didn't even sing. With grateful hearts, *we simply told the Lord how wonderful He is.*

The room filled with an awesome presence and I landed on my face on the grimy carpet. I could hear angel wings whirring above me and shout songs of "Holy! Holy! Holy!"

When finally I dared to rise, I found my friend still sitting on her bed trembling, her eyes glazed over in wonder. "It was like huge hummingbird wings in my face," she exclaimed in wonder.

† **Worship draws us near to God and opens the way to feel His intimate and powerful presence.**

What did Isaiah experience in God's presence? How did he react? Isaiah 6. _____
_____
_____

One time, as I worshiped with other women in a spiritually dark country, the fragrance of rose petals burning filled the room. We searched for the source throughout the house, and even outside, but it was only in the place we worshiped.

Another time, a friend felt the ground tremble and saw God's hand writing in the air, *"I accept your surrender."*

Many other times, we've seen miracles, people healed and other manifestations of God's presence. But *the most powerful experiences I've had with the Lord personally have been in my quiet times alone with Him.*

† **A lifestyle of private worship is key to life and depth in your intimacy with Christ.**

What are your quiet times like? Do you have one every day? How much time do you usually spend?
_____
_____
_____

God is intimate and personal, and every experience with Him is unique. Occasionally, He meets us in astounding ways as in the instances above. But more often,

His touch is so soft we must draw near Him to feel it. James 4:8a.

Has that been your experience too? How?
_____
_____

God wants followers who *love* Him—who long so desperately for Him they seek Him with all their hearts. *Those are the ones who find Him.* Jeremiah 29:11-14.

† **The Lord loves to show His glory to those who long for Him.** Exodus 33:17-23.

One day, as I read about how God showed up in miraculous ways at a church service, I had to put the book down. I didn't want to read about someone else's experiences; *I wanted my own.*

So I headed out alone on a hike in the snowy wilderness asking God to show me His glory.

About a mile out, I was praying and enjoying God's creation when a pack of wolves stepped out of the forest and encircled me.

I froze. "I wanted to *see* Your glory, Lord; not die and *go* to it!" my mind screamed as I begged Him to spare my life.

But then the wolves slipped back into the trees and left me alone. As I hurried up a rise toward safety, the Lord's still small voice whispered in my mind, "Do you want to see My glory? Turn around."

I turned just in time to see the sunset light up

the top of a mountain as if on fire.

Miraculous displays of God's glory are all around us all the time if we would but look for Him.

But sometimes I get so caught up in *how* I want God to answer that I miss *how He answered*. Matthew 16:1-4. I'd seen many sunsets more spectacular than that one in my lifetime. But what other unexpected way did God show me His glory in that snowy wilderness?

_____
_____

Have you ever expected God to do something in a certain way and He didn't? How did that make you feel? What did He do instead?

_____
_____
_____

Whether you feel God's touch or not, whether He answers your prayers the way you want Him to or not, God is still worthy of worship. Job 1:13-21; 13:15; Habakkuk 3:17-18.

So worship Him.

The ways to worship God are as varied as the people He has created. How do you like to show God praise, adoration, reverence and honor?

_____
_____
_____
_____

I may bow, sing, dance, play an instrument, use my own private sign language, read a psalm, paint a picture, write Him letters, songs or poetry.... I not only adore this God I love, I also *enjoy Him*.

† **Worship puts things into perspective and changes the attitude of your heart.**

As you fix your eyes on God, He comes and meets with you in intimate ways. He may pour His love over you, reveal a solution to your problem, show you what He's doing, give you courage, topple lies with His truth, destroy your excuses to sin.... ***Worshiping Him changes everything.***

Read the poem at the beginning of Part 1, and pray back to God whatever touched your heart.

_____
_____
_____

Meditate on Psalm 135, and then spend time worshiping the Lord today. Write your experience with Him here. _____
_____
_____
_____
_____

Expect God

The key to experiencing God is to draw near to Him and believe He will draw near to you. James 4:8. He may not do what you imagine He will, but He will most certainly meet with you when you seek Him. Jeremiah 29:12-14a. If you don't expect Him, though, or if your mind is somewhere else, you may miss the show. Isaiah 55:6.

Delight in the Secret Place

11

Place of power

Deep within the temple of your heart, behind the veil of busy acts of service, is a Holy of Holies where your Lord is waiting to commune with you. It's called the *Secret Place*.

What is the map Jesus gave us to get there? Matthew 6:6? _____
_____

Have you ever done that? Where do you go to get alone with the Lord? _____
_____

Our family travels often because of the work God has called us to, but I like to set up my own little nook wherever we are, a corner where I can go each morning, before anyone else awakens, curl up with a cup of coffee, my Bible and my journal, and *meet with the One I love.*

Each rendezvous is new and exciting. Sometimes He shows me wonders in His Word I never noticed before. Other times I worship or intercede. He may show me sin, set me free from a stronghold (See Chapter 16), give me His holy solution to a problem, rearrange my schedule to match His, help me make a difficult decision, write a book with me (like this one), or flood me with so much peace I fall asleep in His arms.

But it's not a date I can skip. **I long for Him. I need Him. *I can't go a day without Him.***

Do you feel that way too? Why or why not? _____
_____

During that season when my friends were attacking me, Jesus awakened me long before dawn every day. He knew I needed that extra time with Him so His truth and love could wash over me and heal my wounds. I don't know how I would have made it without those early morning dates with my Counselor.

How about you, what are some ways God has met you in the Secret Place? _____
_____
_____
_____

Everyone's journey with the Lord is unique, as is every quiet time. But if you get in the habit of meeting with your Beloved every day, and give Him enough time to speak, *He will transform you, your circumstances and your life forever* through those daily power encounters. And He will also *change the lives of those around you because of what He is doing in you.*

Do you have roommates? Does that make it hard to find a time and place to be alone with God? What did Jesus do about that? Mark 1:35. _____
_____

Jesus often prayed for hours at a time. How do you think that affected His ministry and His relationship with His Father? John 5:19-20. _____
_____
_____

Some mornings I wake up at sunrise and go for a hike or jog with the Lord. If we're in a city, I may prayerwalk, interceding for the neighborhood and people who live and work around us. If we're near natural beauty, I may hike with Him on the beach, up cliffs, through forests, by a lake (Only do this in safe locations, of course, and with others nearby who know where you are.)

I love how He paints the sky in brilliant colors and delights me with wildlife at that time of day. I feel so tiny in the vastness of His beauty, and the power of His presence and whispers of His love take my breath away.

Jesus often withdrew from the crowds, even His

disciples, to be alone with His Father. Luke 5:16. Where did He go? Luke 6:12, Matthew 14:22-23.

What is unique about the view from up high?

In the dark land where we serve, I sometimes hike up to a bird's eye view of lost villages nestled in the valleys below, and yet more scattered across the mountains. As I pray for God to release them from darkness, He shares with me His love, compassion, and vision for how to reach them.

In Luke 21:37, 22:39 and John 7:53-8:1, where did Jesus go to be alone with His Father? What could He see from that vantage point? Mark 13:3. Why do you think that was important?

Your King is calling you to "Come up here" to a place of rest in His presence where you can rise above your circumstances, see through His eyes and know *He's in control, He loves you, and He has a plan.*

That high vantage point is not a physical mountaintop so much as a spiritual placement. He's asking you to lay down your worries, agendas and longings, crawl up into Love's arms and *trust Him*. 1 John 4:16, John 8:31-32.

From that Eagle-eye view of His presence, He may give you instructions. Exodus 24:12. Or meet with you in powerful ways. 1 Kings 19:11. But whatever it is He wants to do when you are alone with Him, *you don't want to miss it.*

In Luke 6:13-16, what decision did Jesus make and what did He do first before making it?

Have you ever done that? Blocked out time alone with the Lord before making a big decision? Why was that important?

In Matthew 14:22-33, what did Jesus do after His time alone on the mountain with His Father?

That's powerful! That same power that *walked on water, calmed the sea, raised the dead and made the blind to see* **lives within you to empower you to do all He did and more.** John 14:12-14.

Whatever the enemy is telling you you're not, whatever he's saying you will never be or do for God, *don't listen to him.* He's working overtime to feed you lies against God's calling on your life—telling you that you're not good enough or not as gifted as so-and-so, that you say or do the wrong thing, that you always mess up and maybe you should just be quiet so others can do it better....

Sound familiar?

Don't let the enemy deceive you. You are not a mistake. **You are a special agent for your King uniquely equipped to shine His beauty and love into the dark and fallen world around you.**

The experiences you're going through now are forming, testing and transforming you uniquely for His purposes to draw you closer to Him and influence others to do the same. **God wants to finish the work He started in you and empower you to push back the darkness with His light.**

You were made for more than the mundane. You were made to be a conduit for His power and love.

So get into the Secret Place and get started!

Plan time for God to lead and empower you

Make a daily habit of entering the Secret Place so God can heal you, transform you and empower you. But also plan times once a week or once a month to spend half a day or more alone with the Lord. (For questions or ideas on what to do in these special times with God, feel free to write MoreThanAConquerorBooks@gmail.com, or message me on Facebook @Mikaela.Vincent.75.)

Delight in Conversing with your King

12

Whatever you ask

Alone with the Lord in the mountainous desert of a war-torn country, I noticed He had inlaid my path with colorful stones stretching for miles, each uncut jewel unique in its shape, size and hue. I gazed in wonder at the blood-reds, dusty violets, dark ebonies, forest greens, crystal whites and lapis blues all crowded together, embedded in the cracked desert floor... and felt God calling me to share His Living Water with parched hearts that thirst for more of Him, each one more precious and beautiful than jewels to the One Who created them.

What an astounding privilege we have to interact with our Creator—to walk with Him, talk with Him, feel His touch, hear His voice, *know His heart* like that, that He would speak to us in such extraordinary ways.

He didn't just toss us out into this world to make it on our own; **He created us for oneness with Him.**

Is your heart parched and thirsty for more of the Lord? Do you know how precious you are to Him? Or do you feel like an overlooked grey slab while others shine in more stunning colors?

_____
_____

Have you had trouble meeting God in deep ways in your quiet times? Or even having a quiet time at all? _____
_____

We've all been there. Even those who walk close to God have seen their share of deserts. Psalm 42.

But if you want your prayer life to turn around, if you want to feel His presence and be empowered by His Spirit to make a difference in the world, ... *start by planning regular dates with your Betrothed.* **Get to know Him. Share your heart with Him.** *Let Him share His with you.*

Your Lord knows your situation. Not only has He been there beside you all along, but He also experienced temptations and hardships Himself.

So *talk* with Him. He has a plan for you, a light at the end of the tunnel He's drawing you toward. But *you have to hold His hand to see your way through the dark without stumbling.* Isaiah 50:10.

Here are some great conversation openers:

* "Lord, delight me with Your love today. Surprise me in some way only You can."
* "Is there anything I'm doing You haven't asked me to do? Or anything You've asked me to do I'm not doing?"
* "Lord, I'm opening the door of my heart to You now. Do anything in there You want."
* "When You look at me, what do You see?"
* "What's on Your heart today? What makes You happy? What makes You sad?"
* "Say anything You want. Show me anything You want me to see."
* "This is what I'm going through.... What are You doing in the midst of all that? Show me so I can join You there."
* "This is what I'm feeling.... What do You say about that? What is Your truth?"

If you're not accustomed to conversing with God, don't be discouraged if you can't "hear" His voice straight away. Just **purpose to draw near.** Take the time to be still before Him. Clear your mind and the space around you of distractions so you can position yourself to listen. And remember He speaks in many ways (See Chapter 13).

The key is your heart. *Are you surrendered?* And *are you listening?* If you are, you won't miss what He has for you. Jeremiah 29:11-14a.

What does Matthew 21:22 say? Do you believe that? Why or why not? _____
_____

In the dark country where we live, we pray each night for the Lord to fill our home with His presence and surround us with His angels, guarding us and all our things from harm.

When a business moved in next door, they began parking their vehicles in our carport instead of theirs. When we asked them why, they said, "Because when we park them in ours they get stolen, but when we park them in yours they don't!"

† **Prayer draws us near to God and releases His power upon the earth.** Revelation 5:8; 8:3-5.

Do you remember a time when God answered a prayer or a question you asked Him? Explain. _____

_____

Almighty God can do anything He wants any time. But He most often waits for us to pray. *He doesn't just want to get something done; He wants to do something with us and in us.*

† **When we pray God's will, we push back the darkness and defeat the enemy's purposes.**

That's why *one of Satan's main schemes is to keep you from praying.*

When we pray, *we join in God's purposes.* We don't just give Him a list of all the things we want Him to do, we *seek Him for what He wants to do.*

If you're not sure what God's will is or how to pray, **try praying His Word.** He already said it, so you know it's His will.

Not only that, but the Word is our "sword," our *offensive weapon against the powers of darkness.* Ephesians 6:10-18.

If you want to pray protection over your family, for example, try Psalm 91. What does verse 1 say about the Secret Place? _____

_____

What are some ways God keeps us safe? (v. 2-16) _____

_____

What does that psalm mean to you?

_____

_____

_____

Write Psalm 91 into a prayer in your journal.

When does Ephesians 6:18 say we should pray? What does that look like for you? Ask the Lord and write what He shows you. _____

_____

_____

What situation do you know of needs prayer? Ask God for His heart on the matter, search the Word for a promise, and then *pray*.

In fact, make two columns in your journal, the left with prayer requests and the right blank for now. As God answers your prayers, write and date how He does that in the right column.

God is always doing something amazing.
Prayer gives me a front row seat and
positions me to be used by Him.
But if I don't pray, I might miss the miracle.

Pray the Word

Get in the habit of looking for promises in the Word and praying those back to God. However the enemy attacks you, he will tremble at the use of your "sword." Luke 4:1-13 (vv 4, 8, 12).

Delight in knowing God's voice

Close to the Shepherd

Read Psalm 23. What kind of a Shepherd is God? _____

What do you gain by following Him? _____

Think about it. You're a sheep (Isaiah 53:6; John 10:1-21), and there's a lion out there. 1 Peter 5:8. Whom would you rather hang out with?

I'm guessing you'll want to stay just as close to your Good Shepherd as possible. Not only does He know where the green pastures are, but *He loves you and fights for you.* 1 Samuel 17:34-35.

The enemy may try to lure you out to the fringes of the flock with a big fat lie-weed. But I promise you, those lies are bitter. And the farther you wander from Jesus' voice, the easier it is to be devoured. Jeremiah 50:6-7; 1 Peter 5:8.

† **Recognizing the Shepherd's voice is crucial to following Him.** John 10:1-5; John 8:31-32.

"He calls his own sheep by name and leads them…. The sheep follow Him, for they know His voice. Yet they will by no means follow a stranger, but will flee from him, for they do not know the voice of strangers." John 10:3b-5

† **You need to know God's voice so intimately that** *all other voices makes you flee to His side.* James 4:7-8; 1 Peter 5:8-9, John 10:1-5.

Many voices compete for your attention. But if you listen to anyone but Jesus, *you could find yourself in the lion's mouth.* Proverbs 3:5; 1 Peter 5:8-11.

The voice of my own **selfish desire** is often the loudest. Jeremiah 17:9. I sometimes get that one mixed up with God's because *I want it so badly I imagine He wants it too.*

The voice of **doubt** says God's not speaking or I must be mistaken. The voice of **reasoning** says, "That can't be right because…." The voice of **experience** decides what's right even before God speaks. The voices of **tradition** and **legalism** drown out God's voice with habits and rules. **Others'** voices sway us, too, especially people we look up to.

Then there's my **enemy.** He likes to tell me what "sounds" true but is cunningly contrary to what God says. I have to be on the alert to notice. John 8:42-47, 2 Corinthians 10:3-5, 1 Peter 5:8.

So, how can I know God's voice?

Whatever God says will agree with His Word and His love, and draw you closer to Him.

† **God communicates with you constantly.** Isaiah 45:19; 50:4-5; Psalm 29; 19:1-6; Romans 1:18-20.

He speaks in different ways. Here are just a few:
- ☐ **The Word** (2 Timothy 3:16-17)
- ☐ **His still, small voice in your heart** (John 14:26, Psalm 42:8, Ezekial 18:1)
- ☐ **Dreams** or **visions** (Acts 2:17)
- ☐ **Impressions** or **urgings** (Acts 15:28)
- ☐ **Circumstances** (2 Corinthians 12:7-10; Psalm 40:1-3)
- ☐ **People** (1 Corinthians 2:4-13)
- ☐ **Nature** (Psalm 125; 19:1-4)
- ☐ A sense of **peace** (John 14:26-27, Philippians 4:4-7, Galatians 5:22)
- ☐ Other: _____

Check the ways God most often speaks to you. Which ways do you wish He would speak more? Why? _____

How did God speak to Moses? Numbers 12:6-8. What was it about Moses that invited the Lord so near? See Numbers 12:3.

† **Humility draws us into God's presence and places us in the right position to hear Him.**

Remember, *humility is agreeing with God.* **Just because I believe something doesn't make it true. Only what God says is true.** When I disagree with Him or rebel against Him in some way, I set myself above Him, *as if I know better than God.*

† **If you learn to tune your ear to God's voice continually, He'll make your every moment a God-awesome one.** Romans 8:28, 35-39; 16:19-20; 1 Corinthians 2:2-5.

Read Hosea 2:14-16. How does God speak in the hard times or "deserts" of life? (v 14)

How does His nearness change our relationship with Him? (v 16)

† **His voice heals you, sets you free.**

He may pour His love over you (Isaiah 54:10); give you new revelations of His truth (Jeremiah 33:3); point out a sin He wants to set you free from (Isaiah 30:15); sympathize with you (Hebrews 4:15-16); guide you (Matthew 10:18-20); or tell you what He's about to do before He does it (Isaiah 42:9).

Is there a circumstance in your life He wants to speak to you through? Is there a sermon you heard that touched your heart? A verse you read that gave you strength? If you haven't written that in your journal, do that now.

And then... Sit still before the One you love. Clear your mind, block out every distraction and *listen to Him.* Write what you feel Him saying, and run it through the Three-Fold Sieve below.

The Three-Fold Sieve

Use this Three-Fold Sieve to know God's voice and distinguish truth from lies:

1. *Does that thought you have right now line up with the Word (all of it, not just a verse or two; even Satan knows Scripture and twists it for his use. See Luke 4:9-13)?*
2. *Does it line up with God's character, especially His love?*
3. *Does it draw you (and others) closer to God?*

Delight in listening to God   14

Want hearing aids?

Do you sometimes feel God is silent? Explain. _____
_____
_____

Just because you can't hear God speaking doesn't mean He's not.

† **God speaks even through silence.**

Try reviewing this checklist with Him to see if something's blocking the way (Isaiah 57:14):

☐ Are you having your quiet times? *If you skip too many days in a row, you'll become more accustomed to other voices than to God's, and your relationship will feel dry.*

☐ Are you positioning yourself to listen? *If your quiet times are too busy or you talk a lot, He may be waiting for you to be still.*

☐ Is your heart clean? *Use the Galatians 5:22-23 Gauge in Chapter 16 to check for unconfessed sin, lies and wrong thought processes so God can set you free. Also, some families where a door has been opened to the enemy through the occult can experience a strong compulsion to bolt or fall asleep whenever God is speaking. Refer to the list and instructions in Chapter 19.*

☐ Do you start your quiet times with prayer, inviting God to be in charge and to guard that time you have together, forbidding any enemy intrusions?

☐ Are you focused? *If your thoughts dart about, making it difficult to stay on track, try turning those thoughts into prayers, asking God what He wants for those situations and people. If you can't stop thinking about a task that needs to get done, keep a notepad handy so you can write that down, and then go back to listening.*

☐ Are you setting aside enough time to be still? *If you're under stress, it may take you longer to quiet your heart. Try blocking out 2-3 hours on your calendar for a "date" with Him; or better yet, take a 2-3 day vacation with God. Is there anything you're busy doing that He never asked you to do? Time with Jesus is more important than accomplishment or busy acts of service. Luke 10:38-42.*

☐ Are you handing your troubles to God and trusting Him? Matthew 6:33. *Even if your eyes are closed and you think you're praying, worry and anxiety are barriers to trust and surrender. You may need to lay down your fears, opinions, hopes and desires before you can hear His heart.*

☐ Are you expecting God to speak? ***If you expect God to speak, you're more likely to hear Him.*** *But if you believe that God doesn't speak or that He speaks to others but not to you; if you dismiss His voice with thoughts like, 'That's just me,' or 'I'll think about that later,' it's like closing the door in His face.*

☐ Are you obeying God? *If you think you're hearing Him but you're not sure, run it through the Three-Fold Sieve. If you're still not sure, try asking Him, "Lord, are You saying such-and-such?" He might confirm it by highlighting a Scripture, speaking encouragement through a friend, or giving you a sense of peace. If you're still not sure, hand what you feel Him saying back over to Him: "Lord, it feels like You're saying thus-and-so. I'm headed that way because I want to obey you. Please make Your will clear."*

☐ Are you asking God questions? Keeping your heart open for Him to speak any way He desires? *If you expect Him to speak with a "voice," you may miss the urgings or impressions He was laying on your heart, or something He said to you through the Word or someone else.*

Try one or more of those suggestions this week. Can you feel God speaking yet? What's He saying?

_____

_____

Another thing I love to do is to ask the Lord to bring songs to mind that He wants to sing over me, or for me to sing to Him. Try that today and write what He says to your heart.

_____

_____

A few years ago, I felt God urging me to teach a Bible study, but whenever I specifically asked Him about it, I heard His voice in my mind say "No."

Confused, I asked Him again, "Do You want me to teach this Bible study this fall?"

"No!" His voice resounded in my mind. "*I want to teach it!*"

I had asked the wrong question! I rephrased it. "Do You want me to be a warm body in the room while *YOU* teach?"

"YES!" came the emphatic reply. That Bible study turned out to be one of the most unforgettable experiences of my life. Every time we got together, God performed miracles and radically transformed us. I'm so glad I listened to that urging and asked Him again, and even more glad *He* was the one Who taught it!

Describe God's voice in Psalm 27. _____

_____

_____

† **God's voice is powerful. It rocks the world and turns wrong thoughts upside down.**

One day, a friend came to my house angry because a woman she didn't like would be at a Thanksgiving gathering and she was sure that woman would "ruin" the event for her family. I encouraged her to worship God and **lay all her** *opinions about that woman at His feet; then ask Him how He sees her.*

He showed her that woman's rejection and pain. By the time my friend left my house, her anger had turned to compassion and love. She exclaimed, "Oh, Mikaela, I can't wait to see her! I just want to hug her and tell her how much God loves her!"

How do you think my friend's Thanksgiving went after that encounter with God?

_____

_____

What might that holiday have been like if she hadn't listened to Him? _____

_____

_____

What a change tuning in to God's voice makes —from anger to joy, and bitterness to love!

What about you? Is there some situation bothering you? Or someone who annoys you?

Play your favorite worship music and focus your mind on the Lord. His holiness. His beauty. His mercy. His love.

Imagine He's there in front of you now. *Because He is.* Bow before Him, and lay all your opinions and ideas about that matter or person at His feet.

Now, ask Him how *He* sees that situation and each of the people involved? Lie still before Him, letting Him cleanse your heart with His truth, and write what He says here. Run it through the Three-Fold Sieve in Chapter 13.

_____

_____

_____

How does that truth change your perspective?

_____

_____

_____

The key to listening is obedience

Don't worry if you feel you can't "hear" God yet. Just keep asking Him questions and looking for His answers. He may speak in an unexpected way, but you'll know it's Him if it lines up with His Word and His love.
The key to listening is obedience. Each time you obey, His voice gets louder.
But disobedience separates you from His felt presence.

Delight in following His lead

Making wise decisions

Can you think of a time when you obeyed the Lord and were glad you did? Explain.
_____
_____

True obedience flows naturally from a passionate love for Christ.

† **The closer you walk with Jesus, the easier it is to obey Him.**

John 14:15 says to my heart: *"If you really love Me, you will have no problem obeying Me because it will be all you want to do!"*

Matthew 22:37-40 joins that verse to do away with long lists of dos and don'ts because *love is our one command.* If you're loving God and loving others, then *you're already doing everything your King asks of you.*

† **Obedience to Christ is to your advantage.**
1 John 5:3-5, Deuteronomy 29:13.

You don't want to miss out. This God Who loves you and created you knows much better than you do what is best for your life. If you head off in your own directions now, driven by what you or other people want, by the time you realize what a mistake you've made, it may be too late. Jeremiah 29:11, Isaiah 55:6-9, Matthew 7:24-27.

God can bring something good out of your wrong choices and messy relationships. But *you really don't want to miss the blessing of a life surrendered to your King.*

What if that amazing man of God He prepared for you passes you by because you're too busy trying to fit in with the crowd, wearing sexy clothes or hanging with the wrong boyfriend to shine like the woman of God he's looking for?

I can't begin to imagine what my life would be like if I hadn't chosen early on to follow Christ. I would have missed out on my man-of-God husband and all the amazing adventures we've had together taking Christ's light into dark corners of the world.

The choices you make now have everything to do with how the rest of your life goes.

Some of my friends who were hungry for more of Jesus gathered together with me each week to seek the Lord. It was an incredible time of worship, as God met with us, taught us from His Word, healed us and set us free....

But when hardships hit, two of those women decided drawing near to God was too costly. They stopped worshiping and praying, even in their own quiet times. Not long after, they fell into sin, their marriages fell apart, and they left the church.

Whether we follow God or not, we will face difficulties in life. The difference for the one who chooses God's path through the trials is that He walks it with us. Matthew 28:20.

† **The more you obey God, the closer you get to Him. The closer you get to Him, the louder His voice is and the easier it is to obey.**

In Proverbs 3:5-6, which decisions are we to seek God for? _____

And when should we lean on our own understanding? _____

When did Jesus do the will of His Father? John 8:29b. _____

Have you ever made decisions based on
☐ what you think is best?
☐ what you want?
☐ fear of what might happen?
☐ fear of what others will think?
☐ pressure from people?

- ☐ time constraints?
- ☐ others' advice?
- ☐ experience?
- ☐ need?
- ☐ accomplishment, ambition?
- ☐ other _____?

How do you usually make big, life decisions?
_____
_____

What about the smaller ones, like when to clean your room, what show to watch, whether or not to go out with your friends?
_____
_____

One leader argued that some decisions must be made fast; no time to pray. But *it only takes one second to pray, "Show me what to do, Lord."*

One second of surrender, *as you seek God and trust Him to guide you in the next,* **can make the whole difference.**

A wise woman knows she can't lean on her own understanding, even if she has all the "facts," because her own wisdom isn't complete.

> *"'My thoughts are not your thoughts, nor are your ways My ways,' says the Lord. 'For as the heavens are higher than the earth, so are My ways higher than your ways, and My thoughts than your thoughts.'"* Isaiah 55:8-9

If you have chosen Christ as your King, then no matter how incapable you feel to do the things He calls you to, know this: ***Wisdom Himself lives within you.*** 1 Corinthians 1:26-30. ***So lean on Him.***

How to make wise decisions:

1. Before you react, before you worry, before you go to someone for advice or help, ***pray.*** *Ask God what He wants to do. Listen to Him.*
2. Make sure you ***know the facts.*** Don't rely on your imaginations about the situation or on mind-reading (assuming hidden motives behind people's actions or words). Research to find out both the truth of what happened and what God's Word says about that.
3. Be willing to be wrong. Your way is not the only way, and may not even be the best way. ***Lay your agendas down*** and ***ask God for His.***
4. Take time to ***listen.*** What is God saying to those who will be affected by your decision? What experience does someone close to the Lord have in that area? ***Pray together with them seeking God's will.***
5. Run others' advice through the Three-Fold Sieve (Chapter 13). ***Only receive what you know God agrees with.*** James 4:11-12.
6. What do you feel God leading you to do? ***Make sure everything you do agrees with Love.*** Matthew 22:37-40, 1 John 4:16.
7. Now ***hand your decision to God*** again. *"Lord, it feels like You're saying..., so I'm headed in that direction. Show me clearly if I'm wrong."*

How different is that method from the way you've normally made decisions?
_____
_____

Let's try the above method now. What decision are you facing? Ask God what He wants to do and follow the steps in this chapter that apply. Write what God shows you. _____
_____
_____

Whatever God asks you to do will always agree with Matthew 22:37-40. Why? _____
_____
_____

Don't lean on your own understanding

Don't just do or think whatever you feel like doing or thinking. Use the Three-fold Sieve to know which voice you're listening to. Don't lean on your own understanding. Seek God in everything and let Him direct your paths. Proverbs 3:5-7. Ask God what He's doing, listen for His answer and join Him there. Isaiah 50:4-5.

You were made for freedom

You were made for freedom.
You were made for this.
You were made to live each day
Empowered by Jesus' kiss.
For He has won the battle.
You've nothing left to fear.
So rest against His chest until
His heartbeat's all you hear.

You were made to soar over
Mountains in the way;
Not to view with earthly eyes
The problems of today.
But riding on His pinions,
You'll see what eagles see—
A land that stretches far beyond
Each earthly boundary.

But if you let the stress and muck
Of all these earthly cares
Stick you to the ground in one
Of Satan's nasty snares,
You'll miss what you were made for,
You'll miss the sweet way out.
Then all of freedom's joy and peace
Will perish in your doubt.

Don't miss what you were made for.
Surrender to His will.
He sees what's up ahead of you,
Each valley, every hill.
This God who knows your future
Knows what's best for you.
So trust Him and you'll conquer,
Not just make it through.

Part 2:
Delight in Freedom, Joy and Abundant Life

Delight in your Counselor

Guardian of the heart

Read John 14:16. What has your Heavenly Father given you that is so precious?

_____

What other names does He have? (14:17, 26)

_____
_____

People pay thousands of dollars for years of therapy with earthly counselors, but seldom are fully healed. You see, no matter how much training or experience a psychologist has,

- **Only God knows your heart.** Psalm 139; 69:5; Matthew 12:25; Mark 12:15; Luke 5:22; 6:8.

He made you. He loves you. He was there with you when you cried those tears. He saw what that person did to you. He heard those ugly words spoken, the blows dealt, and felt your pain.

- **He knows exactly what you're going through.** Genesis 16; Psalm 69:19.

He can see deep inside your heart; He knows why you feel what you feel, and ...

- **He knows how to heal you.** Psalm 30; Psalm 107:10, 20.

His counseling is free!

- **He wants to heal you so you can draw closer to Him and feel His lavish love.** Psalm 41, 42, 107, 103; 142:7.

This Counselor, the Spirit of Truth, is speaking to your heart even now. Can you feel Him?

- **He is with you all the time.** Matthew 28:20; Psalm 139; Joshua 1:5.

God created you so you can know Him and enjoy Him and bring Him glory.

He wants you to walk so closely with Him that *every moment is a love adventure;* to laugh with you in the good times, hold you close in the hard times, and fight for you.

- **He can make even the bad turn out for good through His love for you.** Romans 8:28, 35-39.

A friend asked me for help with a brochure one time, but whenever I gave a suggestion, he spouted off angry words. A need to prove myself rose up inside me, but instead of retaliating with a list of my degrees and experience, I politely excused myself and went into another room to be alone with God.

I asked Him where that negative reaction first entered, and He reminded me how the kids in grade school had bullied me. "I must not be important if you treat me this way," was the lie that surfaced.

Then He flipped my thoughts to a memory of me teaching a handicapped girl how to draw. *Through my pain, He had built in me a need to help others.* Now He wanted to purify that need into *a gift of helps empowered by His Spirit.*

He took me back to the memory from school, only this time I was wearing a royal robe and crown. "You were the only Christian in that class," He said to my heart. *"They should have bowed to Who your Father is."*

God set me free that day. As far as I know, that need to prove myself has never returned.

- **An encounter with Jesus changes you.** Isaiah 55:6-9; John 8:31-32; Isaiah 61:1-3.

Knowing something in your head isn't enough. I already knew I was a daughter of the King. What I needed was for Jesus to speak that truth deep down inside my heart where a lie had taken root and pull it out so I could be free. Psalm 51:6.

- **He can topple a stronghold in one moment of truth.** 2 Corinthians 10:3-5.

A **stronghold** is a *sin or a wrong thought process that controls your actions and reactions in a certain area of your life rather than the Holy Spirit and God's truth.* Those thoughts or sin habits act as barriers to keep you from knowing Christ deeper.

Is there anything like that in your life? Explain.

_____

_____

A single friend in her 30s struggled with a stronghold of rejection. Lining its walls was the lie, "No one wants me. I don't measure up."

When she asked Jesus where that came from, He reminded her that as a little girl her parents doted on her older brother, but criticized her. They even forgot to pick her up after school one day and left her on the street for what felt like hours!

Feeling forlorn and forgotten in that memory, she asked Jesus what He was saying or doing when that happened. *After all, He was there. He saw it. In fact, He's always been there, even when our hearts have imagined He wasn't.*

Suddenly, she saw Him sitting next to her on the curb with His arm around her. "You have always been precious to Me," He said to her heart. Isaiah 42:16b; 43:4a. Years of rejection slipped away in a flood of God's unconditional love and acceptance. John 8:31-32. And she was healed.

> **Jesus is with us all the time, even when bad things happen. Look for Him and what He's doing in the hard times, so the enemy doesn't take you captive with lies.** John 8:32, 42-47.

In difficult situations, it's often easy to see what the enemy's doing—he's harming you, disappointing you, making you angry, sowing distrust....

But *God is up to something good.* If you give in to the enemy's schemes, letting his lies dictate what you think and how you react, you'll miss out on what God is doing. Isaiah 45:2-3. In fact, not only did He set me free from my need to prove myself that day with my angry friend, but He opened up the opportunity for my husband and me to pray together with him for his freedom.

"If the Son makes you free, you shall be free indeed."
John 8:36

What difficult experiences have you endured? Did something come to mind as you read the stories in this chapter? Walk through the Galatians 5:22-23 Gauge with the Lord below and write what He shows you. _____

_____

_____

The Galatians 5:22-23 Gauge

1. *Whenever you feel a negative emotion outside of the fruit of the Spirit, like fear, depression, loneliness, jealousy, etc., excuse yourself from the situation and get alone with the Lord as soon as you can.*

2. *Ask Him when that reaction first began in you (where those lies entered your heart). Be still before Him and let Him show you anything He wants to. 1 Peter 5:7; Psalm 46:10; Isaiah 50:4-5.*

3. *He might take you to a memory (often from childhood). Allow yourself to feel what you felt when that happened. Look for the lies (like, "Everyone's against me," "I have to do it on my own," "I'm trapped," "I can't do this," "I'll never be good enough," etc.) and any inner vows you might have made (like, "I'll never let anyone do that to me again!")*

4. *Then ask Him for His truth. What was He doing when that happened? What does He say to that?* **This is the truth that sets you free, so listen up.** *John 8:31-47. He might show you what He was doing, remind you of a verse, or impress something else on your heart. (Don't worry if He doesn't show you right away, just keep asking Him to do and say anything He wants; He might speak His truth another way, like through His Word, a sermon, a circumstance or another memory.)*

5. *Confirm His truth with the Three-Fold Sieve (Chapter 13), and do a Word Search (Chapter 8) in your next few quiet times, as you learn to walk in the truth. If the old reaction recurs, walk back through these steps again so He can show you any lies or other memories He wants to heal.*

Delight in the Truth
Get rid of those lies!

When I shared with my friend Kaye about God's amazing love, and how He sees us—His bride—as beautiful and perfect because of what Christ has done for us (Chapter 3), she responded, "I have no problem believing Jesus says *you* are beautiful, Mikaela, and that He shows *you* His love. But He doesn't do that for me."

Have you ever thought God does things for others but not for you? Why? _____
_____

When Kaye was younger, her brother told her she was ugly. She looked around at other girls, compared herself to them, and agreed.

Those agreements became the building blocks of strongholds of rejection, fear, and a low self-image—each one acting as a barrier to knowing God deeper. 2 Corinthians 10:3-4.

Spiritually speaking, a "lie" is anything that is contrary to what God says.

In John 8:42-47, who's the liar? _____

Why couldn't the religious leaders accept the truth Jesus spoke to them? (v 43)
_____
_____

The lies we believe are prison walls in our hearts keeping us captive to the enemy. John 8:47. **We need Jesus to set us free.**

How lies can get a hold on us:
- The enemy usually introduces a lie to us through **negative life experiences**.
- Believing and **acting on the lie** (sinning) gives him a foothold. Ephesians 4:27.
- Now that he's invited (you opened the door by agreeing with him rather than God in that matter), **he fortifies the lie** with yet more lies and more negative life experiences to make those lies sound "true."
- Built by lies that set themselves up against the knowledge of God, **strongholds lead us to act and react contrary to the Spirit.** 2 Corinthians 10:3-5, Romans 7:14-25.

According to John 8:31-32, how do we position ourselves for freedom from the lies and strongholds that keep us captive? _____
_____
_____

One great way to know if something you believe is a lie or the truth is to sift your thoughts through the **Three-Fold Sieve** (Chapter 13).

Let's do that right now with Kaye's belief, "Other women are beautiful but I am not."

First, does that agree with the Word? Why or why not? Read Song of Songs 4:7; Hebrews 10:14; and Psalm 139:13-14. _____
_____
_____
_____

Second, does it agree with God's character, especially His love? _____
_____
_____

The One who created us isn't in the business of making junk. Genesis 1:31. He didn't smite us with some self-perceived flaw just to make us suffer. *He loves us* and *handcrafted us in His image*. Genesis 1:26. Even what we see as "flaws" are truly unique, wonderful, and beautiful. Psalm 139:13-14. So if I believe I'm ugly, *my thoughts are the problem, not His creation!*

Third, does believing God made us ugly draw us closer to Him? Explain. _____
_____
_____

It's an eyes issue. Matthew 6:22-23. What does Hebrews 12:2 say we should fix our eyes on?
_____
_____

Instead of looking at ourselves through self-pity or a low self-image (see all the "self" in there?), let's look at Jesus and how amazing our God is.

Often what makes something a lie isn't necessarily that it isn't "true" in an earthly sense, but rather that *our focus is in the wrong place.*

Jesus is Truth. Revelation 19:11; John 14:16. **He is the Truth we fix your gaze on to be free.** Then, whenever I do look at myself, I can look through *His* eyes, not others', the enemy's, or even my own.

I also can't use human logic to decide if something's truly true. Why is that? See Isaiah 55:8-9 and Proverbs 14:12. _____
_____
_____

For example, God says I'm beautiful. So if I say I'm not, I'm disagreeing with Him, *as if I know better than God.* In other words, what man considers "humility" is actually pride in God's eyes.

Now let's look at Kaye's belief that God doesn't show His love to her like He does to others. Ask God the questions in the Three-Fold Sieve in Chapter 13 and write what He shows you:

1. _____
_____
2. _____
_____
3. _____
_____

What thoughts have put up barriers in your own relationship with Christ? Ask the Lord, write what comes to mind, and then run that thought through the Three-Fold Sieve with Him.
_____
_____
_____
_____

What are you looking at?

Humility is agreeing with God and always being aware that you're in the presence of Someone greater than you. *A good way to recognize a lie is by the **focus**. For example, one woman said, "I think we shouldn't think too lowly of ourselves, but we also shouldn't think too highly of ourselves. Somewhere in between is about right." But the problem is, why are we so focused on what we think about ourselves anyway? GOD is the great and glorious one! If my eyes are focused on HIM, then I'm too busy gaping in awe or asking for His viewpoint to think about what I think of myself. ... Get in the habit of* **running your thoughts through the Three-Fold Sieve to make sure they agree with what God says.**

Delight in freedom

Truth that sets you free

Has God revealed a stronghold to you yet? What is He showing you? _____
_____
_____

Take a moment to memorize Galatians 5:22-23 and list the fruit of the Spirit here:

- _____
- _____
- _____
- _____
- _____
- _____
- _____
- _____
- _____

Is there any time in the last few days where you felt something negative outside the fruit of the Spirit? If you're like most of us, it may have been many times and many different emotions. Ask the Lord to show you which one was the strongest and write that emotion or attitude here.
_____

You want to get in the habit of recognizing thoughts and emotions that are contrary to the Spirit, so you can find the strongholds that control you and let the Lord set you free to walk in the fullness of His empowering love.

Today, let's walk through the Galatians 5:22-23 Gauge (Chapter 16) together with the Lord, so you can position yourself for truth to be planted deep in your heart. John 8:31-32.

What was the situation that triggered that negative emotion or attitude? _____
_____

Ask the Lord where that reaction entered your life. When did you first start feeling that way? Invite Him to take you anywhere He wants to take you and show you anything He wants to show you. He may lead you to a memory where that feeling or reaction first began. Don't dismiss what comes to mind, even if it seems trivial or a long time ago. Write the memory here or in your journal.
_____
_____
_____

Focus on remembering and feeling what you felt when that happened. Ask God to show you the lies or vows. Try to express your feelings in sentences. Write what comes to mind.
_____
_____
_____
_____

Jesus was there when that happened. Ask Him what He was doing and saying. Stay in that memory and look around for Him or listen for what He's saying to you. Write what He shows you.
_____
_____
_____

Is there anything else? Don't leave this moment until you're sure He's finished speaking.

Take what you felt the Lord saying to you and run it through the Three-Fold Sieve (Chapter 13) to make sure it's Truth. Write the verification here.

1. _____
   _____
2. _____
   _____
3. _____

For most lies or strongholds God sets you free from, you should notice an immediate sense of lightness, like a burden has been lifted.

Go back into the memory of the more recent event that triggered that negative feeling or reaction. How do you feel about the situation now?

_____
_____
_____

You should feel very different—lighter, *free*. But if there's still a negative impulse there, you can go back through the Galatians 5:22-23 Gauge again to let God expose more lies.

There may also be other things the Lord will ask you to do in the next few days or months to secure your freedom. For instance, He may take you through experiences and scriptures to teach you how to walk in the Spirit in that area of your life.

You can also do a Word Search (Chapter 8) over your next few quiet times to help plant His truth deep in your heart. For instance, if your issue is fear, look up "fear," "panic," "anxious," "worry," "tremble," "afraid," and also the opposites of "faith," "trust," "peace."

What words should you look up regarding the issue God showed you today? Ask Him, write them here, and then let Him take you on an adventure, writing in your journal the verses and messages from the Word that touch you most.

_____
_____
_____

For me, freedom feels like I now have a choice in how I react, like the temptations and impulses that used to trigger my old stronghold are now coming at me from the outside, so all I have to do is flick them away with my sword or shield. Ephesians 6:10-18. Whereas, before God set me free, it felt like I couldn't control my reactions.

So, watch out for situations that trigger that old lie; and ***stand in the truth. The stronger you stand the harder your enemy will fall.*** Ephesians 6:13. After a while those old thoughts won't even come anymore because *freedom will be your new norm* and Satan will give up that fight.

As we went through the Galatians 5:22-23 Gauge today with the Lord, did you notice any vows you might have made?

An **unholy vow** is a form of *self-protection denying God's sovereignty over your life and setting yourself in His place as your protector.* 2 Samuel 22:3. For example, if your parents divorced, you might feel hurt enough to vow, "I'll never get married!" How might the enemy use that vow against you? _____

_____
_____

Can you see how important it would be to break that vow and hand control back over to God?

Pause for a moment and ask the Lord if you've ever made an unholy vow (like, "No one will ever do that to me again!" or "I'll never...."). Repent now and break that vow. You might say something like, "In the name of Jesus, I renounce the vow 'I'll never get married,' and I release my future into God's hands, for I am His. Whatever He wants to do in my life, that's what I want too." Write your renunciation here.

_____
_____
_____
_____
_____
_____

Stop before you react—

*To walk in step with the Spirit, Galatians 5:25, we must lay down our old habits and pick up new ones. Whenever you feel negative reactions rising up within you, seal your mouth shut, close your eyes if you need to, don't worry about what the other person thinks, just **excuse yourself from the situation as fast as you can and go find a place where you can be alone with God**. Ask Him where that reaction first took root in your heart, and let Him tenderly pull up those lie-weeds so He can plant His beautiful truth in their place.*

Delight in breaking ancient chains

Shutting the door on the enemy

Your strongholds affect more than just you.

In fact, one time, as my toddlers argued over a toy, saying, "Mine," the Lord showed me greed in my own heart. As I repented, *their arguing stopped.*

That happened with several other strongholds, revealing this pattern: *Whenever the Lord set me free from a stronghold, my preschoolers were most often released from that sin tendency, as well.* But when they reached a certain age (for my son, it was 5, the age he received Christ), my own repentance wasn't enough; they had to repent, too, to experience freedom.

In other words, **some strongholds are generational**; meaning *we tend to walk in the same issues our family members do.* 1 Kings 15:3, 26; 1 Kings 22:52, Exodus 20:5, 34:6-7, Numbers 14:18, Deuteronomy 5:9, Luke 11:50-51.

Do you have a negative habit that is also an issue for your parents, grandparents or other family members? Ask the Lord and write what comes to mind. _____

_____

Try walking through these steps with the Lord:

1. **Ask God to protect** and lead your time together and to forbid the enemy to interfere.
2. **Repent** of any part you had in that sin, and walk through the Galatians 5:22-23 Gauge to let the Lord **replace any lies with His truth.**
3. **Forgive** that family member who opened the door. Matthew 7:1-5, Proverbs 10:12.
4. **Renounce** the sin. Nehemiah 1:6, Psalm 79:8, Isaiah 61:4 and **cut off any curses.** For example, *"In the name of Jesus I renounce infidelity, and I cut off any curses that have fallen on me or my descendants because of that sin."*
5. **Deal with any demons.** Mark 9:25. *"In the name of Jesus, I send the spirit of infidelity and any other demons attached to it (divorce, distrust, greed, selfishness, lust, seduction, pornography, whatever God shows you), to the feet of Jesus to be dealt with by Him, and I forbid them to ever pick on me, my family, my children or my children's children ever again...."*
6. **Pray opposite blessings** over your family and generations to come; and **for Jesus to be your Shield and Protector.** Ezekial 18, Genesis 17:7-9, Exodus 20:6, Deuteronomy 5:10, 7:9, Psalm 22:30, 24:6, 79:13, Luke 1:50. *"Thank You, Lord, that I am Your child and that Your blood has covered my sin and my bloodline. Protect me, my children, and their children forever from evil attacks regarding infidelity, and bless us with faithfulness and love."*
7. **Keep seeking the Lord each day to walk in freedom.** Galatians 5:1, 25. Use the Galatians 5:22-23 Gauge (Chapter 16), a Word Search (Chapter 8) or anything else He shows you.

A generational sin that was common to the Israelites but also to us today is **occult activity.**

If you or any of your family members have experienced mental illness, suicidal thoughts, freak accidents or illnesses, early death, or overwhelming urges to flee or fall asleep when God is speaking, it's possible a door to demonic activity and a spirit of death has been opened through occult activity.

Even if you're unaware of any such issues, check over the following list, asking the Lord to show you any open doors. Then walk through steps like those above to close them, replacing the underlined words with whatever God shows you.

If He highlights anything on the list, linger there with Him, as there may be other steps He wants you to take to be free. Listen in and obey. Write in your journal whatever He is showing you.

Satan worship	casting spells	potions	prostitution	Black Muslim	cutting the body	Children of God
curses	astrology	acupuncture	prognosticators	Hinduism	graphology	magic healing
apparitions	Moon-many	mysticism	psychography	Taosim	neo-rationalism	Bahaism
black magic/arts	horoscopes	Aryanism	transference	Unity	agnosticism	Eastern Star
black mass	zodiac signs	Humanism	New Age	Mormonism	atheism	Hare Krishna
white magic	icons	psychokinesis	powwow	omens	iridology	hypnotherapy
neutral magic	numerology	telepathy	yin-yang	occult jewelry	reflexology	Roy Masters
séances	parapsychology	psychometry	superstition	shrines, temples	color therapy	Father Divine
clairvoyance	enchantments	mind control	spiritualism	lodges	death magic	soul travel
mediums	clairaudience	second sight	occult literature	blood pacts	firewalking	horoscope charts
divining	unholy dreams	mental science	the force	oaths	fanaticism	eckankar
psychic powers	unholy visions	self-realization	holistic medicine	false cults	Rosicrucianism	offerings to spirits
spiritism	fetishes	visualization		rock music	screening	table tipping
ghosts	runes	trances	levitation	martial arts	witchcraft	good luck charms
necromancy	amulets	yoga	graven images	evil dance	mind science	incense burning
conjuring spirits	talismans	mesmerism	idolatry	voodoo	sorcery	automatic writing
fortune-telling	mascots	auras	planchette	E.S.P.	precognition	Magic Eight Ball
trance diagnosis	unholy medals	reincarnation	self-mutilation	mind reading	autosuggestion	Christian Science
palm reading	ankhs	psychoanalysis	Karma	poltergeists	biofeedback	imaginary friend
tea-leaf reading	spells	wizards	Buddhism	thought control	psychic healing	channeling spirits
crystal balls	incantations	soothsaying	Islam	tattooing	inner voices	concept therapy

Jehovah's Witnesses	Eastern religions	psychocybernetics	holographic images	astral projection
wart or bum charming	spiritual prostitution	letters of protection	E.S.T. (The Forum)	Masters of Wisdom
animism, spirit worship	Theosophical Society	mental suggestion	transactional analysis	handwriting analysis
Science of the Mind	occult movies/TV shows	Umbanda, Macumba	self-help techniques	out-of-body experience
Freemasonry (Masons)	Order of the Arrow	psychic phenomena	esoteric philosophy	humanistic psychology
Swedenborgianism	death wishes/death oaths	metaphysical healing	rebellion against God	Unification Church
Silva Mind Control	psychic involvement	hypnosis, self-hypnosis	observing of the times	The Way International

human or animal sacrifice	contact with familiar spirits	consciousness-expanding through drugs
materialization or apports	rod or pendulum diagnosis	Science of Creative Intelligence
transcendental meditation	consulting spirit guides or mediums	charts with occult significance
communicating with the dead	automatic drawing or composing	vows (See James 5:12; Matt. 5:34-37.)
pact with Satan or a spirit	massage by someone who channels spirits	mental manipulation, mind-swapping
tarot cards or other card laying	dedication to a spirit, Satan or a cult	ancestor worship or veneration

fortune-telling or anything that predicts your future and has advised your life

blood subscriptions (subscribing yourself or your children to the devil)

false or demonic tongues (test by 1 John 4:1-3 and 1 Corinthians 12:3)

remote influence of the subconscious mind of others

incubi and succubae (sexual molestation by an evil spirit)

association with or possession of occult or pagan objects, relics, idols, images, artifacts or anything dedicated to spirits

religion or philosophy that denies the deity or blood atonement of Jesus (liberal theology that teaches salvation without repentance, Modem Theology, rationalistic or intellectual theology that denies the resurrection, the second coming, miracles, answers to prayer, spiritual gifts, the devil, demons, or God)

occult games (Dungeons and Dragons, Clairvoyant, Kabala, Mystic Eye, ESP, Ouija Board, Telepathy, Voodoo, Horoscope, Masters of the Universe, etc.)

initiation rites (into lodges, brotherhoods, shrines, clubs, sororities or fraternities that require taking an oath to uphold a man-made doctrine)

radiesthesia (water witching, dowsing forked sticks or other objects to locate water, oil, minerals, underground sewer, water lines, etc.)

fantasies, obsessions, other associations with vampires, draculas, werewolves or other occultic super-human manifestations

Other: _____

Put an end to the trend

Look for any doors in you or your family line that have been left open to the enemy, and close them.

Delight in blessing

Words with power

How do you describe fresh air or a sunrise to someone who's been trapped in a dungeon her whole life? *You have to experience it.*

But sometimes, like that prisoner, *we think this jail is all there is.* We say things like, "That's just the way I am," or, "That's normal. Everyone struggles with that." Then when someone gives us dynamite to blow the walls down, we say, "I don't need that," or, "That's dangerous."

In addition to our own excuses to not pursue freedom, the enemy can give us a bit of pushback, as well. How did the Israelites experience worse persecution from their slave masters when God set their course for freedom? Exodus 4:29-6:9.

_____

How did they respond to that pushback? (6:9)
_____

If God has shown you a stronghold and you've asked Him to set you free, the enemy may try to put up a fight. It's kind of like cutting off the head of a huge python—the tail keeps on thrashing even though the beast is defeated. Revelation 12:10-12.

So, don't give up. Stand firm. Ephesians 6:10-14, Galatians 5:1. Jesus is showing you the way out. 1 Corinthians 10:13. *Take it!*

If you're still having trouble hearing from God, ask Him to reveal and remove any barriers blocking out His voice (Chapter 14). Then keep looking for His answers and listening, ready to obey.

Here are ways to help you **walk in freedom**:

† **Look for "the way out" in each temptation.** 1 Corinthians 10:13.

† **What the enemy is doing? Do the opposite.**

† **Ask God what He's doing and join Him.**

† **Don't skip a quiet time.**

† **Use the Galatians 5:22-23 Gauge** (Chapter 16 and 18) regularly.

† Do **Word Searches** (Chapter 8) on the subjects God is teaching you.

† **Keep a journal** so you can return to the truth when you need it.

† **Write the truth God shows you, especially scripture verses, on cards and put them in places you look each day**, like your refrigerator or mirror. *Let the truth you know become the truth you live.*

† **Ask God to help you. The more you resist the lies, the less often they return**, until you find you just don't think that way anymore.

In the Word, vows, curses and blessings were serious business. You can do a Word Search (Chapter 8) if you'd like to know more. But *our words carry power*, whether we think they do or not.

We need to get in the habit of speaking blessings over ourselves and others.

What negative things have you said about yourself? Ask God to remind you and write what comes to mind. _____
_____
_____
_____

One of the ways the enemy picks on us is through *curses we speak over ourselves*. Exclamations like, "I hate my breasts (hair, thighs, nose, fat, etc.)," "My hips are so big," "I'm starving to death," "I'm dying," even if you're laughing when you say it, may open a door for the enemy to fulfill that negative proclamation (breast cancer, freak accidents, etc.). Scary to think about, isn't it?

But what if you speak truth over yourself?

What if the things you say agree with what God says? What if you thank Him for the beautiful gift (of hair, breasts, etc.) He's given you? Not only will your heart come back in step with the Spirit, Galatians 5:22-25, but you will invite heaven's blessings to pour out over yourself and your situation.

Look back at something negative you've said about yourself. Is that true? Run it through the Three-Fold Sieve (Chapter 13) to find out. What does God say about you?

_____
_____
_____

Ask God what other curses you might have spoken over yourself and spend some time with Him breaking those and speaking blessings over yourself with a thankful heart instead.

For example, *"In Jesus' name, I renounce my words, 'I hate my hair,' and break off any curses or any rights the enemy feels he has to pick on me because of those words. I thank You, Lord, for covering me, and for giving me this beautiful hair as a sign of that covering (1 Corinthians 11:15). Truly, I am wonderfully made, for You are the One Who made me (Psalm 139:13-14). Use my hair for Your glory any way You desire, Lord. I am Yours, and I choose to believe what You say about my hair, not what my enemy wants me to believe or say. Restore to me the joy that is mine in You (Galatians 5:22)."*

Write your prayers in your journal as a record of what curses you've broken off and blessings you've proclaimed.

What negative things have you said about others? About your siblings, friends, acquaintances, church, pastor, worship leader, etc.? Ask God to remind you, and write those in your journal.

Read James 4:11-12, and write what He says to your heart here. _____
_____
_____
_____

Ask the Lord to forgive you for any slander or judgment. Matthew 7:1-5. Then cut off those curses, marking them out in your journal as you bless those people and pray for them.

Others have spoken curses over you, as well, perhaps without realizing it. Ask God to show you those, and then walk through this process:

1. Is anything that person said about you true? **Repent**, and if it's something you feel needs the *Galatians 5:22-23* Gauge, do that.
2. If what they said was false or an accusation on your character because of some way you stand for Christ, your accusers are in a precarious place before Holy God. **Forgive** them and **intercede** for them. Luke 23:34. Ask the Lord to show them mercy. Pray for Him to convict their hearts and give them a hunger for Him.
3. Renounce and **cut off the curse.**
4. Then **speak opposite, positive blessings** over yourself and generations to come.
5. Ask God to be a Shield around you, **turning every curse spoken against you into a blessing.** Deuteronomy 23:5.

As you go through the next few days, notice the way you say things, and re-word your thoughts positively. For instance, instead of saying, "I hate that!" you can say, "What an adventure!" or "Life's never boring, is it?"

If you hear others saying bad things about someone, ask God how to counter it, either with something positive and good, or by telling them, "That's not actually true because...." Ecclesiastes 7:21-22.

Blessing or curse?

Judgment, slander and bitterness will lead you down a dangerous road. Matthew 7:1-5, James 4:11-12. Instead, invite God to do something beautiful in every situation. Speak truth, love and blessings, not judgment or curses. Look for God's viewpoint and for what He's wanting to do; then come in line with that. Ephesians 4:15-16, Proverbs 26:2. And always pray for those who curse you. Romans 12:9-21.

Delight in your Savior

Damsel in distress

Imagine you are in a dungeon in the depths of an enemy stronghold. You try every which way you can to escape, but to no avail.

At last, the King you are betrothed to dons His shining armor, fights off your enemies with a whoosh of His mighty sword, and tosses you the keys. You open those heavy doors and race into daylight, heart throbbing with joy.

Your Beloved lifts you up onto the back of His mighty steed. You laugh as the wind whips your hair and your arms clasp about the One you love. Together, you gallop away into open spaces to live happily forever after.

Describe your Rescuer in Psalm 45. _____
_____
_____

What does He fight against? (v 5) _____
_____
_____

What does He fight on behalf of? (v 4) _____
_____
_____

You are in a battle, and the battlefield is your mind.

If you leave your King's arms to reach for a lie, you may find yourself captured and controlled by something other than the Spirit of Truth. John 8:42-47, 14:15-17.

For example, if you believe "I can't do anything right," then, try though you may to do well at whatever, you'll just make a mess of things again and again, because *the enemy loves to confirm the lies you believe.*

But *if you believe Philippians 4:13, and let God empower you in all you do, then you will be more than a conqueror.* Romans 8:37.

"Stand fast therefore in the liberty by which Christ has made us free, and do not be entangled again with a yoke of bondage." Galatians 5:1.

Describe the battle in Romans 7:21-24. _____
_____

Have you ever said about some flaw in your character, "That's just the way I am?" What was it?
_____
_____

Is it possible to change? How? See Romans 8:5.
_____
_____

Strongholds *(sins and wrong thought processes that control your reactions rather than the Spirit)* **keep you from the deeper things of Christ and the abundant life you were created for.** Galatians 5:16-25; 2 Corinthians 10:3-5; John 10:10.

As you can see, **the enemy has much at stake should Jesus bust you out of jail!** He likes to add extra **fortification** to your prison walls through justifications like

- "Everyone's doing it."
- "That's how God made me."
- "It's normal. Everyone struggles with this."
- "I have rights, you know!"
- "Just one more time, and then I'll quit."
- "I'm no worse than that other person."
- "I'll never change."
- "I'm right, after all!"
- "It's not my fault."
- "I'm just like my mom."
- "I need it!"
- "Well, you…!" (pointing at someone else)

Like whitewash covering over the darkness, my strongholds were so heavily guarded by some of the lies on that list that *I didn't even know I was a captive.* Then Jesus gently exposed them to me one by one, and rescued me. *Now I am free!*

Pride was at the center of it all, but I couldn't see it, because I wasn't boastful or mean. Still, when a girl pointed her finger at my nose and said, "You're proud!" I said, "I'll pray about that." And I did.

I went on a quest, asking those I look up to in Christ, "What's humility? What's pride?" Everyone had a different answer, but something was still missing. You see, *man's definitions and God's definitions can often be quite different.*

So I did a Word Search for all the verses with "pride," "proud," "haughty," "meek," "humble," and "humility" in them. That's when God opened up a new definition to me—a heavenly one:

__Humility is complete surrender to God.__ It is fixing my eyes on Him, never forgetting I'm in the presence of One vastly greater and holier than I, seeing my sin as He sees it, repenting, bringing my thoughts in line with His, agreeing with Him, and leaning on Him in complete submission and obedience through every situation all the time.

Suddenly I could see how very prideful I was! What about you? Are you able to do all those things all the time in that paragraph above? Why or why not? _____

_____

Finally, He reminded me of all the times He had brought people into my life so I could share Christ with them; but I didn't *because I was afraid of what they would think of me.* That did it! *I hated my pride.* Those prison walls exploded that very night, as I fell on my face before my holy God in repentance, and *He set me free.*

That was many years ago. Pride still tempts me, but I'm not its slave anymore; *it doesn't control me.*

Pride had opened a door for the enemy to build other connected strongholds, like **fear of man** (Galatians 1:10; Colossians 3:23; Jeremiah 17:5; Deuteronomy 1:17; Acts 5:29) **judgment** (Matthew 7:1-5; Luke 6:37; 1 Corinthians 4:3-5; James 4:11-12, 5:9; Romans 14:10-13), **vanity, over-eating, a deep need for people to love me, fear, rejection, desire**, and the list goes on.

But Jesus set me free from those, as well. My King, wielding His sword on behalf of **truth** (tearing down my self-protective lies), **humility** (giving me courage to surrender), and **righteousness** (bringing me back into right relationship with Him), fought for me, and won! Psalm 45:4.

Now I desire to do God's will, and when I do it there is such joy. Psalm 119:32. *I want to live every moment in the arms of the One I love and for Him.*

Do any of the justifying lies on the bulleted list in this chapter sound familiar to you? Which ones? What sin are you making excuses for?
_____
_____

No pointing fingers!

Pointing a finger at someone else ("I wouldn't be this way if it wasn't for...," "Well, she...") is the best way to miss what God's doing in you. He might just bring around similar trials again and again, until you finally choose to look inside yourself and let Him show you what the real problem is. Yourself. Surrender now and let your Savior set you free!

Delight in your way out

22

Journey to freedom

When you chose Jesus as your Savior, He wiped away your sin. In fact, you have been made perfect now because of His sacrifice. Hebrews 10:14, Matthew 5:48. If sin is what He saved you from, then *why do you keep on sinning?*

Look at the second part of Hebrews 10:14. What is He still in the process of doing in you?

You are on a journey to draw closer to the One you love and to be set apart as holy unto Him.

It's not a road without hard knocks. You have a real enemy who's out to get you. 1 Peter 5:8. He wants to steal all that is yours in Christ and stop you from becoming the beautiful woman of God you are meant to be.

"The thief does not come except to steal, and to kill, and to destroy. I have come that they may have life, and that they may have it more abundantly." John 10:10

- **Jesus gives abundant life.**

Read Galatians 5:19-24. What abundant life "fruit" in verses 22-23 do you feel you're lacking?

_____
_____
_____
_____

Do you see in yourself any of the sins in verses 19-21? What other sins do you struggle with?

_____
_____
_____
_____

- **Sin blocks you from experiencing the fullness of all that is yours in Christ.**

Read Romans 7:19 and describe the struggle.

_____
_____
_____
_____

Do you feel like that sometimes? Like the sin itself is in control of you? Romans 7:20. Explain.

_____
_____
_____
_____

- **Whenever you give in to sin, you set yourself up for a slippery slide into captivity.**

It's as if chains snapped onto your wrists. Romans 6:16-23. Before you know it, the enemy has built an entire fortress around your jail cell to make sure you don't break free. Ephesians 4:27. You try to stop doing that same old sin, but it feels impossible. You promise God, "I won't do it anymore!" But, bam! You fall again.

- **Your will isn't strong enough to bust down prison walls.** *You need Someone stronger.*

Jesus holds the keys. Let Him show you what's in your heart so He can set you free.

If you are captive to a sin, the walls of your prison cell are built with lies—thoughts and inner beliefs that led you into that sin. John 8:42-47.

For instance, if you let jealousy control you, your bricks might stack this way: "I wish I had such-and-such.… How come everyone else gets to have that and I don't? … She has it too.… I'm telling others how awful she is."

Did you see how quickly jealousy led to judgment, slander, and revenge?

If you give in to one sin, you invite more.

Then before you know it, you've sentenced yourself to a lifetime of joy-killing strongholds.

But what if, when you feel that pang of jealousy, rather than feeding those thoughts, you confess them and ask for help: "Jesus, I'm so sorry. I did it again. Why am I so jealous?"

He may lead you to take your eyes off what you wish you had and worship Him, … or He may remind you of all the incredible things He's given you, replacing greed with thankfulness, … or He may lead you to pray for and bless the person who triggers that jealousy in you.

He might even remind you of a time when you were young and a sibling got something you didn't. Maybe the lies went something like this: "Mom and Dad like him better than me," or "I always get the hand-me-downs."

When you ask Jesus for His truth, He might remind you how beloved you are and show you how much He has lavishly given you.

Everyone's journey to freedom is different. Just follow wherever He leads. Listen to His urgings, dig into the Word, and let Him show you the way out He's made just for you.

- **Freedom removes the barriers and brings you closer to Jesus, so you can feel His love and walk in peace and joy.**

Do I sound like I know what I'm talking about? I do. I've been inside prison walls so thick Jesus had to tear them down brick by brick.

But now that He has set me free, I am no longer a slave to those thoughts and sins. And let me tell you, *freedom is sweet*. I can choose to do the right thing, and *do it*. The temptation might still come, but the struggle is over, because the lies that built my dungeon are gone. I know the Truth now, I love Him, and *He has set me free*. John 8:31-32.

- **When Jesus sets you free, you are free indeed! John 8:36.**

Ask God to show you any sin you're captive to, and what thought processes lead you there. Choose to repent. I find it helps to see the ways my sin hurts God and others so I will **hate it so much and be so repulsed by it I never want to do it again**. Ask God to forgive you and to set you free.

Now, let God speak truth to your lies. Walk through the Galatians 5:22-23 Gauge in Chapter 16 or do a Word Search (Chapter 8).

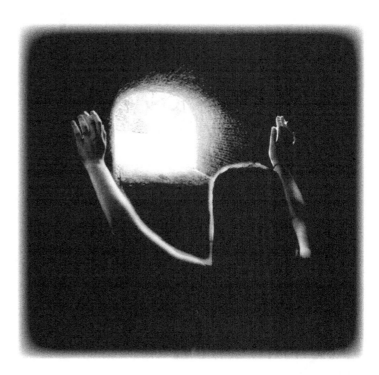

Take the way out

Want to be free. *That's really the first step to freedom.* ***Want it badly enough to do whatever it takes to get there.*** *Let God show you the "way out" (1 Corinthians 10:13) each time your old way of acting or thinking crops back up, and then follow Him there. If you fall, let God teach you through your mistakes, then next time watch out for those thoughts that led you to the fall. Rather than responding as your flesh wants to,* ***excuse yourself from the situation as fast as you can and get alone with the Lord so He can wash you with His Word and change you.*** *Ephesians 5:25b-26. (See the Galatians 5:22-23 Gauge in Chapter 8.)*

Delight in your focus

Eyes only for Him

Right now, you're reading this paragraph. You can see there are other paragraphs surrounding it, but your focus is on this paragraph. You know there are objects and furniture in the room, and maybe even some activity going on, but those things are not your focus. This paragraph is.

It's kind of like that when you fix your eyes on Jesus. Hebrews 12:1-2. You are in the midst of people and circumstances and you go through them, but *your focus is Jesus.*

You're looking for what God's doing, how you can bring Him glory, what He's saying through this circumstance, ... *and that changes everything!*

One morning, some friends and I felt God leading us to hike to a certain village in the country where we live. We loaded up on water, but it didn't last long. After many hours of picking our way through the jungle over steep mountains, we realized we were lost.

We could have given way to fear, anger, dissension or blame. But instead we worshiped God. As the sun went down and the stars came out, we trusted Him to sustain us and guide us, even if we spent the night in the jungle.

At last, around 10 p.m., a man passed by and took us to his village. As his family and neighbors gathered around, we shared with them the Good News about the God who loves them. It was their first time to ever hear. In fact, *until that night, they didn't even know God existed, much less Jesus.*

We faced many difficulties that day—thirst, hunger, fear, discomfort—but **the journey God had planned for us was more important than the destination.**

To God, *we weren't the ones who were lost, that village was.* And **our meeting that man was a God appointment.**

Sometimes you might be headed toward a goal, even a Godly one, but things get in the way. So you're frustrated, disappointed, discouraged. You might even get angry at God for not doing what you thought He would. But if you remain in those thought processes that pull you down, *you could miss what God's doing through that interruption.*

What hardships are you facing these days? Is there anything that's not working out quite the way you planned? _____
_____
_____
_____

What do you think the enemy might be doing in the midst of your difficulty? _____
_____
_____
_____
_____

Knowing these basic truths about God can help open your eyes to see what Jesus is doing during your trials (Proverbs 19:21; Isaiah 46:10; Romans 8:28, I Peter, Psalm 119, and well, the entire Word!):

- † God is in control.
- † Nothing happens, not even the hard things, unless God allows it.
- † If He allows it, then it is because He is doing something good.
- † Whatever good He might be doing in others' lives through your trials,
- † **He is always drawing you closer to Himself.**
- † The quicker you surrender to God and step in line with whatever He's doing, the quicker the enemy and his purposes will be defeated.
- † Obeying God brings peace, rest and joy, even in the midst of chaos.

What do you feel God might be doing through

your present trials? _____
_____
_____

It's okay if you don't know the answer yet. I often don't know all He did until the whole trial is over. But *if you are surrendered to Him and ask Him to lead you through the hard times, He will bring you in line with what He's doing.* You won't miss it.

And no matter what good things God might be doing in the situation and in others, you can always be sure **this trial is about Him drawing you closer to Himself.** So get started. Draw near to Him. James 4:8.

Here's another pointer:

Even if you can't see what God is doing, purpose to do the opposite of what the enemy is doing.

If you're angry at your friend, *lay all your opinions and ideas at Jesus' feet and ask Him to let you see her through His eyes.*

He may want to show you something in your own heart that is an issue. Are you judging her? Are you guilty in some way of the same sin? Matthew 7:1-5. Rather than lashing out at her and saying ugly things, *forgive her, pray for her and bless her.* Romans 12:9-21.

If you're depressed, don't stay in bed with the covers over your head. *Worship.* Psalm 40:1-3.

Rather than complain, *thank God.* Let Him turn your mess into His best. Philippians 2:14, 4:4-9; Romans 8:28.

If you see some way you've given in to enemy schemes through this trial, *choose now to get back on the Lord's track.*

God is bigger than your messes and will even make something beautiful out of them if you let Him.

Is there anything you need to repent of? Anyone you need to ask forgiveness? Write what you feel Him leading you to do. _____
_____
_____

"Where the Spirit of the Lord is, there is freedom."
2 Corinthians 3:17 (NIV)

Whether you're facing a trial at the moment or not, it's still easy for the enemy to slip in and bend you to his purposes.

For instance, he could keep you so busy (even doing good things) that you stop having a quiet time with the Lord.

Or he could distract you with thoughts of how much you don't like a certain song so you end up focusing on that during church, rather than focusing on the God you went there to worship.

Ask the Lord to show you any way you have given in to something the enemy wants you to do or think. Write what He shows you and repent.

_____
_____

What can you do that is opposite to what the enemy is doing? _____
_____
_____

Write God a prayer asking Him to help you see what He's doing in your life right now so you can do that together with Him. _____
_____
_____
_____
_____

Sometimes the only reason you can't see what God is doing is because *you didn't ask.* James 4:1-3.

Do the opposite

Sometimes during trials, it's not easy to see what the Lord is doing. But what the enemy is doing is obvious. He's discouraging you, making you angry, dividing a friendship.... So, even if you can't see what God's doing yet, **purpose to do the opposite of what the enemy is doing.** *And know that whatever great things the Lord has planned that you can't see yet,* **God is always drawing you closer to Himself.** *So draw close to Him.*

Delight in Surrender   24

Just say "Yes"!

Name some things you're afraid God will ask you to do that you don't want to do.

_____
_____
_____

Fill in the blanks of the thoughts below you can relate to:

☐ "I'll go anywhere You want to send me, Lord, but not _____."

☐ "I'll be anything You want me to be, but not _____."

☐ "I'll do anything You want me to do, but not _____."

Have you ever made a decision without praying first because you were afraid of what God might say? What happened? _____
_____
_____

When I was in tenth grade, I remember sitting under the stars in our front yard, with my Siamese cat curled up in my lap, telling God all my ideas about future careers.

I liked music, art and writing, but nursing was at the bottom of my list. When others hurt, I hurt too. What a depressing career that would be, crying all the time, with no time to do the fun things I loved!

But then, the One who made me and loves me more than I love myself skipped over all my delightful career choices and got straight to the bottom of my issue: "I want you to be a nurse," He said.

I choked. He had to be kidding! But no, the feeling persisted. For three months I struggled against those words, with self-pitiful tears.

And then finally one night, I crawled back out under the stars before Him and surrendered: "Lord, I love You. My life is Yours. If You want me to be a nurse, I'll be a nurse."

I can't describe to you the peace that flooded my soul that night. I could almost touch His delight and hear His laughter.

And then—*how I love what He does with "and then" after my heart is finally surrendered to Him!*—He led me to get a degree in writing instead.

Oh, He didn't lie to me. Throughout my life, He has used me to heal hundreds of people, but through *His* power, not human knowledge. My ability to cry with those who hurt became a gift He used to open up others' hearts to Himself so He could heal them in the inmost places. Psalm 51.

You see, more than a career, more than my service to Him, more even than my obedience, *He wanted my heart.*

When love is what compels you to surrender, then obeying Him brings joy, peace and abundant life.
Psalm 119.

Plus, *God loves you and is for you.* He's omniscient, so He knows your heart and your future. **His plans for you are not only good, but *spectacular.*** Jeremiah 29:11; John 10:10.

How can you know God's will? After all, there's no verse in the Bible that says, "Mikaela, I want you to be a writer."

The closer you walk with God, the clearer His will for you becomes.

Sometimes, the very reason His will is not clear yet is because **He wants you to seek Him**. Isaiah 55:6-9. You see, He loves relationship. *Anything He asks you to do is to draw you closer to Him.*

So, *get on with it! Spend time with Jesus!*

Here are some basic steps you might take to **walk in God's Will**:

1. **Clear away the barriers.**

    Ask God to show you what is plugging up the ears of your heart. As long as doubt, fear, selfishness, pride, or any other sin or wrong thought process rules in you, it could act as a barrier to hearing His voice clearly. Romans 12:2.

2. **Lay everything at His feet.**

    Tell God your thoughts and feelings. Lay before Him the pros and cons of the options you have. Be honest with Him, even if it's to say, "Lord, please don't ask me to _____."

    What did Jesus Himself ask for in Luke 22:42?
    _____
    _____
    _____

3. **Surrender to God's will.**

    Like Jesus, tell God you are willing to do whatever He asks of you, even if it doesn't feel fun.

    Read Hebrews 12:1-3. What emotion did Jesus feel as He went through with what God had planned for Him (v 2)? _____

    When you surrender to the Lord, you too will feel joy and peace. *There is no sweeter place to be than in the center of His will.*

4. **Ask God to show you His will.**

    Did you notice I asked you to *surrender first* to His will, *even before He has told you what that is?*

    Don't keep saying to yourself, "God doesn't talk to me." He's talking to you all the time. *He just doesn't use the same loud voice the enemy and the people around you do.*

    What do you feel God asking you to do? Does it line up with His Word and His character? Is there a verse that's given you comfort or peace recently? Is there a Bible character who faced something similar? Those are some good ways to know what His will is.

    God is not keeping secrets from you so you will flounder around in the dark and make big mistakes. Isaiah 45:19, 48:16. He is *for* you. If you walk close to Him and surrender to His will *He won't let you miss it.*

    But remember, you are on a journey. *Lying at His feet in surrender, trusting Him even when you can't see or hear Him, may be the very thing He is asking you to do far above making the actual decision you're asking Him about.*

5. **Check for red flags.**

    Do mature believers disagree with your decision? Why? Is there anything in Scripture contrary to what you want to do? Is a door closed, something barring you from moving forward in the direction you want to go? Have you asked Him to open it if it's His will? Do you lack peace when you think of that decision you're about to make?

6. **Obey.**

    Step out in faith, moving in the direction you feel led to go. Pray, "God, it feels like You want me to…. So I'm heading that way. If this is not what You're asking me to do, make that clear. Close the doors, give me a verse, speak clearly, whatever You want to do. I want to follow You."

    What decision or difficulty are you facing these days? Do you trust God in that situation? Is surrendering to God hard for you? Why or why not?
    _____
    _____
    _____
    _____

    Follow the process outlined in this chapter. Write what you say to God and what you feel Him saying to you. _____
    _____
    _____
    _____
    _____
    _____
    _____
    _____

Winning through surrender

It is always to your advantage to surrender to God. He is for you, even more than you are!

Delight in faith

He's the Man!

25

What makes you anxious or afraid?
_____
_____
_____

What do these passages say about God's power?

Isaiah 42:13: _____
_____

Philippians 4:13: _____
_____

Psalm 18: _____
_____

Psalm 27:1: _____
_____

God is all-powerful.

He is greater than your greatest fears, stronger than your powerful foe, mightier than an army.

Write Matthew 10:28 in your own words.
_____
_____
_____
_____

This God who is Almighty, just, loving and faithful is the fearsome One—not a bee, a person, a mistake, or even a demon. Deuteronomy 10:20-21.

God is in control.

Over and over in His Word, the Lord says, *"Do not be afraid."* Why? Isn't once enough? What does Deuteronomy 7:17-24 say to your heart?
_____
_____
_____

Everyone must bow to the Lord (Isaiah 45:23), **and even the enemy is subject to Him.**
James 2:19, Isaiah 54:16-17.

Check out James 2:19. What are demons afraid of? _____

Unlike the demons, you're in a great position:

The One who is in control loves you and wants what is best for your life.

Write Romans 8:31-39 in your own words.
_____
_____
_____
_____

If all-powerful God loves us and is on our side; if nothing can separate us from His love, and we are more than conquerors through Him…

Then why are we still afraid sometimes?

We're in a battle. 1 Peter 5:8-9.

Take a look at Ephesians 6:10-18. What do we fight against? _____
_____
_____

What is our spiritual armor in this battle?
- The belt of _____
- The breastplate of _____
- The shoes of _____
- The shield of _____
- The helmet of _____
- The sword of _____

A fully-armored soldier on full alert (1 Peter 5:8-9) **with blazing sword outstretched and a massive shield covering her whole body is an intimidating sight to the enemy.**

What does 2 Corinthians 10:3-5 say we are to demolish in this spiritual battle? _____
_____
_____

How are fearful thoughts against the knowledge of God? See Isaiah 35:4; 41:10; 54:17.
_____
_____
_____

So how do we take fearful thoughts captive and hand them over to Christ? See Philippians 4:6-7.
_____
_____
_____
_____

And what does that passage say God will fill you with in place of fear? _____

In 1 John 4:18, what casts out fear? _____

In 2 Timothy 1:7, what does God give us instead of fear? _____

What does 1 Peter 5:7 say we should do with our anxieties? Why? _____
_____
_____

You can trust God.

He alone knows what is best for your life. You can't see what's around that bend in the road, but He can. And as much as you want to protect yourself from whatever dangers are lurking about, *you will never be as strong or as wise as the Almighty who is your Shield*. Psalm 18 and 91.

When you bow to fear, you miss out on the joy and rest that come from faith and trust. Isaiah 30:15. And if you try your own ways of self-protection (like defensiveness, avoidance, vengeance, slander, gossip, rebellion, etc.), you may miss out on the good plans God has for you. Jeremiah 29:11.

One of the most common fears is fear of man. Are you afraid of what people will say or think? Do you avoid certain people or situations? Do you imagine what others are thinking and then react to them according to those mind-reads? What ways have you built up self-protective walls or made decisions to speak or not speak based on fear?
_____
_____
_____

Ask God when those fears first began. As He shows you a memory or situation, remember your reactions and feelings. Look for the lies, and write them here. _____
_____
_____

Now, hand your fear to Him and ask Him to speak His truth deep into your heart. Write what He shows you. _____
_____
_____

Memorize Philippians 4:6-7 and pray that verse back to Him. Thank Him for being your Shield and Protector. Ask Him to flood your heart with peace, to guide you in each situation, to conquer your fear with His love, and to build your faith so you will obey Him instead of fear.

The Word of God is a lethal weapon against your enemy. Ephesians 6:17, Revelation 1:16. If you're to be more than a conqueror in this moment-by-moment war that is life (Romans 8:37), you need to get a handle on your sword. ***Know what God says and hold onto it no matter what.***

Love casts out fear

Ask God to show you all your fears (like, "fear of being alone," "fear of failure," "fear of being noticed," etc.). Make a list of those in your journal. Then ask Him for His truth (like "God is always with me," "I can do all things through Christ Who strengthens me," "I'm created to shine for God and draw attention to His glory, not to me," etc.). He might show you straight away or He may take longer to walk you through different experiences and His Word to plant His truth deep in your heart. As He does, mark out the fear with an "X," and to the right of it write the way His perfect love casts it out. 1 John 4:18. Ask God to empower you to walk in that truth.

Delight in Victory

26

More than a conqueror

Read Isaiah 43:18-19. What does God ask you to do? Why? _____
_____

Do you believe those verses are for you? Why or why not? _____
_____
_____

Read Philippians 3:12-14. In order to reach for the "prize" that is ours in Christ, what must we do? See verse 13b. _____
_____

Read Romans 12:2. What does God want to do to our minds? Why? _____
_____
_____

There's a reason why we've been working through letting God heal your heart and tear down the lie-bricks of strongholds like fear.

You are in a battle, and the battlefield is *your mind*. 2 Corinthians 10:3-5.

If you let things that happened in the past control the decisions you make today, you'll get beaten up, knocked down, taken captive. Isaiah 1:5-6. And you'll miss the victory that is yours in Christ.

Read Romans 8:31-39. What does verse 37 say we are? How do we become that? _____
_____
_____

*You were made to thrive, not just to survive;
to conquer in battle, not just to get shot at.
John 10:10; Psalm 18:28-40.*

Let's take a moment and picture the battle scene. Read Joshua 1:7-9. What does God tell your heart? _____
_____

Are you alone in the fight? _____

Read Revelation 19:11-16. Who leads the armies? _____

Name the names given Him. _____
_____
_____

What does He look like? _____
_____
_____

Who rides with Him? See verse 14. _____
_____

Read Isaiah 42, a prophecy of Christ. What is His purpose? (v 6-7) _____
_____

And how do you fit into that list of what He is fighting for? _____
_____
_____

What is your job while He fights? (v 10-13) _____
_____
_____

How does that compare with Isaiah 30:29-32? _____
_____
_____

Are you fighting too? See Psalm 149:6-9. How?
_____
_____
_____

Worship is powerful, especially in the battlefield of your mind. ***When you fix your eyes on Jesus, the battle over your heart is won.***

Read Ephesians 6:10-17. Keep picturing this battle with me. What are you wearing?
_____
_____
_____
_____

Look again at your armor. It's not made of metal, is it? Of course not. Metal dinks and bends. In this spiritual battle, you need something impenetrable.

Search through the following verses. What do these pieces of your armor have in common?

† *Truth.* John 14:6.
† *Righteousness.* 1 Corinthians 1:30.
† *Peace.* Ephesians 2:14.
† *Shield.* Psalm 3:3.
† *Salvation.* Psalm 27:1.
† *Word.* John 1:1, 14; Hebrews 4:12.

They are all names for_____.

What does Romans 13:14 tell you to put on?
_____

That's some pretty powerful armor, isn't it?

Okay. So, again, whom are you fighting against in this life? Ephesians 6:10-12. _____
_____
_____

What empowers you to win? Romans 8:37-39.
_____

What do we demolish? 2 Corinthians 10:3-6.
_____
_____

Read Romans 8:5-6, and describe the transformation that happens in our minds.
_____
_____

Whose mind can you have? 1 Corinthians 2:16.

Do you want that? Ask Him for it. _____
_____
_____
_____

Read Psalm 46:10 and Exodus 14:14. What do these verses say to your heart? _____
_____
_____

What are some things in your mind that need transforming? Romans 12:2. _____
_____
_____

Spend time in worship today, asking God to fight for you, to tear down strongholds and to clothe you with the opposite quality that is Christ. Colossians 3:1-14.
_____
_____
_____
_____
_____
_____
_____

Let God win the fight in you

You can do some things to win in this battle—love God with a passion, worship Him, listen when He convicts you of sin, repent, obey. But ultimately, **the battle belongs to the Lord.** *2 Chronicles 20:15.* **Ask Him to tear down your pride,** *self-defense, unforgiveness, anger, or whatever else is keeping you from walking in His Spirit; and to replace it with the opposite quality that looks like Him—humility, sacrifice, grace, mercy....*

Delight in the Spirit   27

What are you full of?

While prayer walking in a closed country, my friend felt compelled by the Spirit to go down a certain street, where he happened upon a funeral. He walked through the open door, laid his hands on the corpse, prayed, and the dead man sat up, *alive!*

Filled with the Spirit, you are powerful indeed—not in your own strength, but in God's.

The Spirit gives the power to heal, topple strongholds, lead people to faith, break down walls of prejudice, move a situation from bad to good, and even change the world in some way.

Have you ever met Christians who overflow with the Spirit? When they speak, you feel Him speaking. When they worship, you feel Him moving. As they walk through life, lives are changed all around them. How did they get that way?

If you live surrendered to God, then His Spirit will flow through you. And if you expect Him to show up, He just might leave you awestruck.

So many people block out the movement of the Spirit because they're afraid of being too emotional or out-of-control, imagining things that aren't real or giving control over to Satan. Have you ever thought something like that? Explain.

_____
_____
_____

God is gentleman enough that *if you don't want Him to do something miraculous or speak to you or through you, He just might not.* Matthew 9:23-25.

God is most likely to show up in power where believers expect Him to.

Some Christians believe that if you speak in tongues, then you're filled with the Spirit; and if you can't, then you aren't. But I've met Christians who boast about speaking in tongues but are bitter and hateful toward others. And I've met others without that gift who are loving and humble, drawing many people to God.

The proof of being filled with the Spirit is not in the gift, but in the fruit. Galatians 5:22-25.

Think about it. When you apply pressure to a spray can, what comes out? *Whatever's in the can.*

So if anger, pride, self-defense, bitterness, self-pity or something else is what you're full of, that's what comes out under pressure.

What about you? What came out of you last time you felt pressured? _____
_____

Do you want to be so full of the Spirit that when stress hits, out comes love, joy, peace, patience and whatever Jesus is doing? _____

Invite Jesus into your space every moment.

I like to begin each day, even before I get out of bed, by asking God what He wants to do and arranging my schedule accordingly. I make sure to plan plenty of time for my quiet time, and then continue in conversation with Him throughout the day, letting Him lead me wherever He's going and use me any way He desires.

Walking with Christ like that didn't happen overnight, though. *I had to build those habits into my lifestyle.* I had to *choose* to walk in the Spirit and *invite Him* to fill me and guide me.

One morning, as I awoke in the dark country where we work, I asked the Lord as always, "What do You want to do today?"

His answer came more specific than usual. At 8:30 a.m. I was to call Isaiah, take a bus to his town to meet him at 11, and then take him to a certain village.

Reason rose up in me. So, I argued, "But Isaiah doesn't even know me; he just knows my husband. Besides, I'm a woman, so we'll need someone else to accompany us. And anyway, no one in that village will be there. They'll all be at the festival going on in another town."

But I surrendered to God all the same. At 8:30, I called Isaiah, half hoping he wouldn't answer. But he did, and by 11, I was telling him face-to-face about the family in that village where two had come to Christ.

"You want me to go there with you, don't you?" he asked. Then he stood up, grabbed his backpack, and reached for his hidden stash of tracts, asking, "What do we take with us?"

Reason spoke out again: "They can't read and write, so we could just take some fruit." Besides, carrying religious materials was dangerous in that country; we could be arrested, or worse.

Then the Holy Spirit convicted me, and I blurted out, "No! *Pray*, and then take whatever *GOD* tells you to take." He stuffed some booklets into his backpack.

As we stood on the street waiting for our ride, two girls who looked like prostitutes approached and asked to go with us. Isaiah explained to me that the night before, as his friend tried to get one of the girls to sleep with him, Isaiah told her, "You don't want to do that," and then led her to Christ.

So the girl and her friend joined us. We arrived at the village just in time to see a daughter I'd never met (because she attended school in another village) and six of her classmates preparing to go to the festival. We asked them, "While you're getting ready, can we tell you a story?"

They listened as we shared with them stories of God's love from creation all the way through Christ. All seven girls came to the Lord that day, plus the friend of the new believer that came with us! And *every one of them could read.*

When Isaiah opened his backpack, he had *exactly enough booklets for each of them* on growing as new believers.

At every turn throughout the day—calling Isaiah, following God's time schedule, trusting Him to provide others to travel with us, going to that village even though I thought the family wouldn't be there, taking dangerous materials—I had the choice to be led by the Spirit or my flesh and reason. *The consequences were eternal.*

God commands us in Ephesians 5:18b to be

_____.

Why is it important to let the Spirit take the lead? Colossians 1:28-29, 1 Corinthians 2:4-5.

_____

_____

_____

In this book, I've written about some pretty radical experiences with God. But I didn't walk into that relationship with Him overnight. It's a journey. Learning to walk in the Spirit starts with the decisions you make right now. If you take the time to practice the suggestions written at the end of each chapter and build them into your daily lifestyle as habits, *you will walk in the Spirit.* But it takes a lot of practice to build a new habit. So don't get discouraged if you fall. Just let God pick you back up and put you back on track.

Anything the Spirit leads you to do must line up with the Word and God's character and draw people to Him (See Chapter 13.)

Spend time in worship today, laying all your responsibilities at Jesus' feet and asking Him to guide you, fill you and speak through you.

Step into His empowering

Get in the habit of surrendering to God every day, all the time and on every matter. Proverbs 3:5-6. Let Him fill you with His Spirit, so when the enemy "presses your buttons," **all that comes out is Jesus.** *The more you listen to God, the closer you walk with Him and the more you surrender to His leadership, the more His Spirit will flow through you to touch others around you. Don't be surprised if He uses you for one of His miracles.*
All things are possible with God, after all. Matthew 19:26, John 14:12.

Delight in higher heights

Soaring high

Did you know eagles can soar *above a storm,* in the blue sky and sunshine, *missing it altogether?* I want to be like that, don't you? I want to break through those clouds and soar high above every stormy trial in life, rather than getting beaten up by the hail, wind, and sleet down here on the ground.

In Deuteronomy 32:11, what does God compare Himself to? _____

What does that verse mean to you?

_____
_____
_____

Sometimes I feel like that baby eagle. I get shoved out of my comfort zone and down I go.

You see, most of us don't know how to "fly" yet. Do you? What did you do last time someone said something ugly to you, or things didn't work out the way you planned? Did you say, "Oh, goody! This is so fun"?

What does James 1:2 say we can feel in trials?

_____

How do we get there?

One way is to let Daddy Eagle swoop down, catch us, and carry us. Write Deuteronomy 1:31 in your own words. _____
_____
_____

Where does He carry us? See Exodus 19:4.

_____

Everything in your life is about God.

You were created to know Him, to love Him, to feel His great love for you, and to bring Him glory all the days of your life. That means,

When trials come, if you think it's all about you, your rough time will only get rougher.

Self-pity is a nasty trap, and so is **self-defense.** *That's a lot of "self" that can make your ordeal worse than it was to begin with.*

But eagles can look directly at the sun. They have a special membrane that protects their eyes. The same is true of us. If we look at the Son when we go through life's storms, His love lifts us up out of the mess that was all up in our face down here on the ground, and He gives us a new perspective—His.

That's what I call "Come-up-here" moments. Sometimes in my quiet times, when I'm crying out to the Lord about some problem that's all up in my face, He says, "Come up here!"

He takes me to His Eagle-eye vantage point to show me what He's doing through it all—how He's changing me, changing others, putting things into place for something yet to come.

Or He reminds me I'm not alone in my trials, that many who walked before me also endured difficulties, and others who come behind me will as well. Hebrews 12:1-2. He might show me events in history and how He's drawing all peoples to Himself.

Suddenly, my problem feels so tiny, yet so important. *It's something temporary I must go through as a part of a much greater plan God is weaving throughout history and the universe.*

Look around the room. Is there a painting or a picture? Get up close and focus just on one little pebble in that picture, so close that it's all you see.

Now step away and look at the whole picture. If you only focus on the pebble, thinking how hard, boring or depressingly grey it is, *you will miss the bigger picture. You'll miss why each stone must be there in order to complete the beauty.*

Come-up-here moments give you God's perspective on difficulties, and provide the courage you need to continue on in whatever He's asked you to do.

Why is that? Read Romans 8:31-39. What is it that we can always rely on about God?

_____

_____

So, whenever you're going through a hard time, and you feel God is far away or that He's not listening, is that true? Why or why not? See Psalm 139.

_____

_____

"Why do you say . . . 'My way is hidden from the Lord, and my just claim is passed over by my God'? Have you not known? Have you not heard? ... He gives power to the weak, and to those who have no might He increases strength… Those who wait on the Lord shall renew their strength. They shall mount up with wings like eagles." Isaiah 40:27-31

Do you want to soar above circumstances on His wings of love and freedom? Here are some tips:

† **Worship God.** Psalm 18. Take your eyes off your problem and remember His greatness.
† **Thank Him.** Philippians 4:6-7.
† Ask Him to open your eyes to see whatever He wants to show you. 2 Kings 6:15-17.
† **Trust Him.** Psalm 20:7-8; 94:18-19.
† **Obey Him.** James 1:22-25; Isaiah 55:6-9.
† **Hand Him every thought.** 2 Corinthians 10:3-5.
† **Listen for His answers.**

Dig into the Word. Look up all the verses related to your trial. Is there something in your heart He's cleaning out? How does He want to change you? Go through this storm riding on the Eagle's shoulders. Deuteronomy 32:11.

† No matter what He's doing in the midst of this difficulty, *God is always drawing you closer to Himself.* So, **make conscious choices to draw near to Him.** James 4:8. (Chapter 29)

Spend some time worshiping God today. Thank Him for all the blessings He's given. What trial are you facing now? Sit quietly before Him, laying your trial at His feet. Ask Him to pull you up to see things from His perspective. What's He doing with it? If you don't feel Him showing you anything, read 1 Peter. Write what He shows you.

_____

_____

_____

_____

Every trial has a purpose in God's plan. And *His plan is always to draw you closer to Himself.* **Don't waste your trials running from Him, because** *He's your ride out!*

Come up here!

Whatever hard times you're going through, sit still before the Lord, handing Him all your feelings and struggles. Then ask Him for His perspective, so you can see from His wide-angle viewpoint.

Delight in deeper depths

Touching His face

Think of a word picture to describe your walk with God. Is it like a desert? A roller coaster? A mountain? A garden? Something else? Explain.
_____
_____
_____

What would you like it to be like? Why?
_____
_____
_____

When we allow God to renew our minds and set us free from sin and thought processes that lead us away from Him (2 Corinthians 10:3-5) *we get more of Him.*

But as long as you excuse away your sin rather than repent (See Chapter 21), it's like trying to hug Him across a mound of garbage. Touching Him intimately feels out of reach with all that smelly stuff in the way.

Sin forms a barrier between you and God. It keeps you from the deeper things.

Walking in the Spirit is difficult when your feet are stuck in muck. You're likely to feel so far away from God you miss what His whisper is saying.

He can reach through your junk to touch you, heal you and speak to your heart. He's like that.

But if you don't let Him clear away the garbage, you'll miss out on the deeper things you were made for—smelling good (2 Corinthians 2:15) and enjoying intimacy with Him all the time.

The joy of freedom from sin and lies is that His voice gets louder, His presence thicker. *Constantly feeling His love and touch becomes the norm. No more roller coaster rides. Every moment becomes a top-of-the-mountain God-moment because your whole heart is His.*

The thoughts that used to depress you can't anymore because your mind is not fixed on self-pity, but on the One who loves you and works everything for the good. Romans 8:28-39.

This abundant life—set free from loneliness, hurt, and everything else that pulls you down in the dumps—is what you were made for.

You were made to dance, with heaven wide open in each down-to-earth experience; to sing, embraced in the arms of the One who gave His life so you could live abundantly. John 10:10.

If you are not experiencing Him like that, maybe there are still some roadblocks.

Try these heart-cleansing steps to freedom and deeper intimacy with Christ:

1. **Love the Lord with a passion.** Make Him your first thought when you wake, your last thought when you sleep, and all your thoughts in between. Deuteronomy 6:5.
2. **Worship.** When you take your mind off your troubles and focus on the Lord, He makes all things clear (Chapter 9). He fights for you and renews your mind. Psalm 149; Isaiah 52:8-10; Romans 12:1-2. Ask God to lead you to the worship songs He has for this season you're in; then spend time in your quiet times soaking in His presence, focusing on Him, and worshiping Him any way you desire.
3. **Open your heart** to God. Ask Him to show you anything blocking you from deeper depths, and be willing for Him to remove that barrier. Hosea 5:6; Isaiah 57:14-21.
4. **Want to be free.** Ask God to show you what your life could be like without that sin or thought process. Decide you want that. Psalm 142:7; John 8:34-36. Step forward into it together with Him.
5. **Look for the entry point.** Ask God, "When did

depression first set in?" He may remind you of something that happened a long time ago. *If the sun went down on your anger without forgiveness, the enemy may have gotten a foothold that needs dislodging.* Ephesians 4:26-27, 31.

6. **Look for the lies.** Ephesians 4:25. Allow yourself to feel what you feel, even if you know it's wrong; and then *lay those feelings before God,* asking Him to show you the lies. *If a lie is grounded in your heart, you will find yourself acting out of that wrong thought process and making decisions because of it.* **Lies must be toppled for Jesus to be Lord of all of your life.** John 8:42-47, 2 Corinthians 10:3-5.

7. **Ask God for the truth.** John 8:12, 31-32. What does He say about what you're going through or thinking? **Spend time in the Word.** Psalm 107:10, 14, 20. (Chapter 8). Sometimes His truth sets you free in an instant, and other times He builds one truth purposefully upon another. Ephesians 5:26-27; Psalm 119:32.

8. **Forgive.** Ephesians 4:31-32. (Chapter 36) Say, "I forgive (person's name) for (action done against you)." Then bless and intercede. Romans 12:9-21; Luke 6:27-31, 37.

9. **Cancel unholy vows.** (See Chapter 18.) Vows can bind your feet to a path outside your Shield. *"Lord, please forgive me for vowing…. In Your name, I renounce and cancel that vow, and I cut off any effects it has had on my life. My life is in Your hands, for You alone are my Protector. I want to do whatever You want me to do."* Ecclesiastes 5:1-7.

10. **Repent.** If God has exposed a sin, don't fight Him, and don't excuse it. Let Him show you how He sees it—how it hurts others or affects your relationship with Him. *The more your sin repulses you, the easier it is to turn from it.*

11. **Look for the Lord in every situation.** If God has highlighted a stronghold, He will bring situations into your life to help set you free. Walk closely with Him through each trial, listening to His voice and obeying. Allow yourself grace to stumble. But learn from your mistakes. Galatians 5:1; Joshua 1:9.

12. **Surrender.** Whatever God wants to do in your life, let Him do it. Proverbs 3:5-6.

Did God highlight any of those suggestions as you read through them? In your quiet times, walk through those, and write in your journal what God is showing you. As He sets you free from lies, notice how close you feel to Him. Listen for His voice. It should be much clearer now. Make constant choices to walk in freedom, like conversing with God all day long.

Clear the way

Draw near to God and He will draw near to you. James 4:8. But if your quiet times feel dry and you go more than three days without feeling God's presence or hearing His voice, look for strongholds, lies and wrong thought processes in the way, and then ask God to help you clear those out. Isaiah 57:14.

You were made for love

You were made for love, dear.
You were made for this.
You were made to feel the joy
Of Jesus' tender kiss;
To let His love flow through you
To others all around,
A never-ending spring within
Of love that knows no bound.

You were made to snuggle in
His infinite embrace,
Your heart so near to His, you feel
His breath upon your face.
You were made to see the flame
Burning in His eyes,
His fiery passion for His bride,
For you, His jewel, His prize.

Now loving the unlovely
Is something you can do.
It's easy to forgive because
He's first forgiven you.
Now that you're accepted,
Now that you are His,
Love with all His love in you.
You were made for this.

Part 3:
Delight in Heavenly Love for Earthly Relationships

Delight in loving

30

Doing what matters most

Who are some of your best friends? What is it about them that makes them such great friends?

_____
_____
_____

God has given me some extraordinary friendships in this life. I can be silly or weird or my words can come out all wrong, but they love me. They don't judge me or look down on me.

A good friend knows my heart and loves me as I am.

They say good things about me behind my back; and when I mess up, they forgive me, pray with me, fight for me, and help me stand.

I've also had some friendships that didn't turn out so well. Whenever a misunderstanding occurred, they were unwilling to work it out. It takes two to have a friendship, after all.

In Proverbs 17:17, what does a true friend do?

_____
_____

A true friend is there for you in the hard times and in the good.

What command does God give us in 2 John 6?

_____
_____

In Matthew 22:37-40, Jesus divided that command into two parts. What are they?

1. _____
2. _____

I love those verses, because they say to me,

If I love God and love others, then I've done everything I'm supposed to do!

Why is love so important?

- **Love is what God is all about.** 1 John 4:7-8.

Think about it. Without God, love wouldn't exist, because *He IS Love*. 1 John 4:7-8, 16.

In fact, love is the reason He created you. He wants an intimate relationship with you so you can know Him and be known by Him, love Him and be loved by Him. Then, through that love, you also can love others and draw them to Him.

- **Love is what this life is for.** 1 John 3:14.

Not only does love make difficult decisions clearer, the hard times easier to go through, and the good times all the better, but …

- **Love helps me break free from my strongholds.** 1 John 4:18; 1 Peter 4:8.

Say, my friend is angry and accuses me. If I walk in a stronghold of anger, I might get angry and accuse her back.

If fear is my issue, I might cower during that confrontation, and then avoid her.

Rejection might send me home with the pain of one more ended friendship.

Self-pity might cry, "Why do people always treat me this way?"

Self-defense might join up with accusation, denial and blame, yelling, "I didn't do that! It was your fault. You…."

But how would Love respond? _____
_____
_____

- **Love listens** (James 1:19-20), **forgives** (Mark 11:25), **speaks the truth** (Ephesians 4:15, 25), and **asks forgiveness** (Matthew 5:23-24).

When I bow to the One whose name is Love, I say "No!" to those other "idols" (strongholds). *My mind is on loving God and loving my friend, not on myself and my self-protective feelings or needs.*

Did you recognize yourself in that negative list

of responses to an accusing friend? It's okay. I've been there too. Going through difficulties in relationships is a great way to expose things in our hearts we might otherwise never see.

But don't stop with seeing it. *Hand it to the Lord and let Him set you free.* (See Chapters 16-19.)

You weren't made to get beat up in the fight. And you weren't made to beat others up. You were made to conquer!

How? What does love do in these verses?

1 Peter 4:8 _____

Romans 12:10 _____

Romans 12:9, 17-21 _____

1 John 4:18 _____

And that's just the beginning of love's power!

As a child, my daughter had a dream she was worshiping Jesus before His throne, surrounded by thousands of people. She called out to them to bow to Him, too, and they did.

But then Satan stood beside her. "Stop telling me lies!" she said to him. "You think you're so powerful, but if you bow to Jesus, He'll give you the greatest power of all—*the power of LOVE.*"

Even the smallest child who walks in Love is more powerful than Satan and all his demons!

❧ **Love conquers all.** Romans 8:35-39

Write your own version of 1 Corinthians 12:31-13:3, inserting the gifts or good things you do for God that amount to nothing without love. _____

What can you do this week to show love to a relative or friend? Ask God to show you how to love that person as He does. Write what He shows you.

_____

_____

What was the last argument you had with someone? Did you defend your actions, protect yourself, avoid the issue, lash back? Did you do anything that might have made things worse?

_____

_____

_____

Is there anything you need to ask God or others forgiveness for? Read James 1:19-27. Write a prayer asking Jesus to fill you with His love so you do what He is doing, rather than what the enemy wants you to.

_____

_____

_____

_____

_____

_____

Love is the only way

If you ever don't know what to do, pick the most loving path. If you don't know what that is, ask, "Jesus, what would You do?" Remember, if you're loving God and loving others, you're doing everything He's asked you to. Matthew 22:37-40. Through His love, you are more than a conqueror. Romans 8:35-39.

Delight in love's Source

Let's go for a swim!

What are ways you love to be loved?
_____
_____
_____

Are those ways you also show love to others? Why or why not? _____
_____
_____

Each person has a different "love box." The walls of that box say, *"If you love me, you will...."*

Do you do that sometimes? Expect someone to love you a certain way, and if he/she doesn't, you don't feel loved? Explain. _____
_____
_____

The problem with our love boxes is they are *self-sized,* built through life lessons we've learned about what we think true love is.

And that's one reason so many relationships break up. One person feels, "If you love me, you'll keep your promises," while the other says, "If you love me you'll overlook my faults."

You get the drift. Most people don't set out to hurt someone they love, it just happens.

If everyone has a different definition of love, then I want God's. After all, ***His name is Love.***
1 John 4:16.

So, when a friend challenged me that something I did in love wasn't loving, I took a dive into the Word, looking up all the Scriptures on love, and letting my King's definitions wash over me. I found this truth there in the pages of His love letters:

With God's love there are no "boxes." His love is *boundless*.

Throughout the Bible, He demonstrates His love in different ways in different circumstances. Sometimes He rescues; sometimes He doesn't. He speaks kindly to one sinner and harshly to another.

The only way to love each individual person heaven's way is to root myself in Love so He flows through me. 1 John 4:16-19.

If I try to love my own way or in my own strength, I'll fall short. For one thing, I'm weak. I also don't know what's in that other person's heart. But God does. He knows just what each of us needs at just the precise moment.

If I draw from love's Source, then He is the One who nourishes, empowers, and leads me.

Read Romans 12:14-21. How is it possible to bless those who persecute you and love your enemies? See Philippians 4:13. _____
_____
_____

When thieves broke into my friend Graciela's home, she offered them lunch. How is that like Romans 12:14, 20-21? _____
_____
_____
_____

She also prayed for those enemies and sang worship songs to God as they tore her house apart looking for money.

So thick was His peace and love in that home, as a matter of fact, that her children actually fell asleep despite the ropes binding their hands and feet. The thief appointed to guard Graciela was so amazed, a door was opened in his heart for her to encourage him to leave his life of thieving and embrace Jesus' love.

Graciela could love her enemies because *Jesus loved her first.* 1 John 3:1; 4:16-19.

His love is more than enough.

When you are like a cup under the faucet of God's love, He flows into you, fills you up, and then overflows out of you, splashing onto the other "dishes" in the sink around you.

Have you positioned yourself under the "faucet"? Or are you still sitting on the counter, dry and scummed with the residue of the last person who "used" you?

If you keep on lashing out at others in anger or retreating from them in fear, without letting God heal the places in your heart that make you act that way, you'll miss out on the joy and peace that are yours in Christ. And everyone around you will miss out too!

So ask God to fill you with His love. James 1:22-25. *Don't miss your quiet times with Him, or you may miss the very empowering or the very answer you need to face whatever's headed your way today.*

Here's another great way to position yourself for a constant flow of His love:

Surround yourself with life-giving friendships.

1. Join a Bible study.
2. Look for someone mature to mentor you.
3. Hang with Godly friends who will
   † challenge you to go deeper in Christ.
   † worship with you.
   † pray with you.
   † share with you the things God's doing in their hearts and lives.

Those who love God and walk in obedience to Him will be the most faithful, life-giving friendships you'll ever find on this earth. Because they too want to love His way.

Read 1 Corinthians 13:4-8a. What are some characteristics of true love?

1. _____
2. _____
3. _____
4. _____
5. _____
6. _____
7. _____
8. _____
9. _____
10. _____
11. _____
12. _____
13. _____
14. _____
15. _____
16. _____

Mark with a star each of the ways above God has loved you. How have others loved you? Write their initials in the margin next to that trait. Now circle the traits you need to work on to love others better yourself. Ask Jesus to fill your empty spaces with His boundless love and overflow out of you to those around you.

Does God have a someone in mind to mentor you? Ask Him. Are there any other Godly relationships or Bible studies He wants you to be involved in? _____
_____
_____

Drink deep of God's love

The secret to loving well is to immerse yourself in the fountain of God's love. A tree with a tap root that drinks deeply from God's love will never dry out, and will produce the fruit of love in all seasons.
Jeremiah 17:7-8; Psalm 1:3; Galatians 5:22-23.

Delight in abiding in Love

Confidence to stand

Is anyone pressuring you to do something you feel is wrong? How do they justify it, saying it's okay to do? _____
_____

It's hard to say "no" to someone you care about or are afraid of. But *what if the very people who should be encouraging you to do what's right are the ones pressuring you to sin?*

Read Ephesians 6:10-18. Remember, you're in a battle. Who is your enemy? Is it people? (v 12) _____
_____

What one word is used four times to describe your stance in the face of the enemy? (v 10-14) _____

Look at Jesus' example in Luke 4:1-13. Satan even quoted Scripture (v 10) trying to trick Jesus. But He stood strong. Where did His replies come from? (vv 4, 8, 12) _____

"If you abide in My Word, you are My disciples indeed. And you shall know the Truth, and the Truth shall make you free." John 8:31-32

Jesus didn't just say it, *He lived it.*

To "abide in the Word" means to connect yourself to Christ constantly, for *He Himself is the Word and the Truth that sets you free!*
John 1:1, 14; Revelation 19:11-13, John 14:6.

Abiding in the Word isn't just reading words on a page. You have a *living* relationship with the Word of God. *The Word is alive and active in you.* Hebrews 4:12. So **let the truth you KNOW be the truth you LIVE!** James 1:22.

To *live* in the Word, you must *draw all your life from Him.* You can't really afford to miss your quiet times and only read the Bible on Sundays. **The Word is your lifeline.** *If you let go of it, you'll fall!*

So, take your Sword into battle with you, (Ephesians 6:17) because giving in to temptation, even just once, can bind your feet to a slippery slide into captivity. James 1:14-15.

How many girls do you know have sacrificed their virginity because some boy talked them into it? Romans 12:1-2.

If you walk closely to your Bridegroom, and let His boundless love fill all the empty spaces of your heart, then you will have the confidence you need in the face of temptation to just say "no."

When my best friends of ten years tried to persuade me to do things against God's Word, I chose not to, and they kicked me out of their group.

Was it unloving for me to say no? *No.*

🎵 ***Love takes a stand against evil and encourages what is good.*** Romans 12:9, 21.

There's so much joy in obeying the Lord. I can't please everyone anyway. Even if I compromise on one thing today, there will just be a new thing tomorrow someone will ask me to compromise on.

So I can listen to my friends, love them, seek to understand them, and point them to the truth; but *I don't have to bow to their idols.*

Read Galatians 1:10, and re-write it in your own words here. _____
_____
_____

Say you're a high school student going out with some friends. You know it's time to head home, but they want to go somewhere else. They urge you to put your cell phone on silent, so if your parents try to call, you won't hear it.

If your parents didn't give you a certain time to be home, you're not really disobeying them by staying out late, right? And if they tried to call you, you really wouldn't know, so you're not really lying when you say you didn't hear the phone, right? Lying would be wrong, after all. Leviticus 19:11.

And yet, *something inside you warns you not to follow your friends' advice.* John 14:16-17, 26. That's the active Word at work in you! Hebrews 4:12.

If you abide in Christ (John 15:1-17), what does He give you to help you make decisions that agree with the Word? See John 14:15-17, 26.

_____

Look at verse 27. What does your heart gain?

_____

In this case, how does calling your parents to ask them first before staying out later agree with Matthew 22:37-40? See Exodus 20:12.

_____
_____

> *Knowing the Word of God and living it brings peace and freedom.* Psalm 119:32.

But doing things man's way can lead to captivity. Proverbs 14:12; John 8:31-32, 42-47.

What if the pressure and the temptation feel so strong you don't know what to do? What does 1 Corinthians 10:13 say? _____
_____
_____
_____
_____

Be strong and courageous. Joshua 1:9. *There is always a way out, so look for it and march that way, even if you're the only one doing it!*

In your quiet time today, look up "joy" in a concordance (there are several online) and read some of the scriptures listed in Psalms. Write whatever you feel God saying to your heart.

_____
_____
_____

Now, answer this question: What would you say to a friend who tells you, "I don't want to be a Christian because Christians don't have any fun"?

_____
_____
_____

Is there any way you have compromised lately or given in to doing something you know you shouldn't do? Explain.

_____
_____
_____

Write a prayer, asking God to fill you with His Spirit and overflow out of you, so your thoughts become His thoughts, your words His, and your actions as He would do them through you today.

_____
_____
_____
_____
_____
_____

Know who you are

The key to standing strong when others try to sway you is to **know who you are in Christ and live it.** *Matthew 6:33.*

† *Before you are a friend of those you hang with,* **you are a friend of Christ.** *John 15:14-15.*

† *Before you are the bride of an earthly man,* **you are the bride of Christ.** *Revelation 19:6-8.*

† *Before you are a student,* **you are a disciple of Christ.** *John 8:31-32.*

† *Before you are a worker,* **you are a servant of Christ.** *1 Peter 2:16; 1 Corinthians 4:1.*

† *Before you are an earthly sister and daughter,* **you are Christ's sister and the daughter of the Most High.** *Mark 3:35; Romans 8:16-17.*

Delight in truthfulness 33

Inside out

Read Ephesians 4:22-25. What does God want you to put off? _____
_____
_____
_____

What does He want you to put on? _____
_____
_____
_____
_____

Write verse 25 in your own words. _____
_____
_____
_____

What does Colossians 3:9-10 have in common with this verse? _____
_____
_____

Satan is the father of all lies. John 8:44. So it's not just your integrity that's at stake when you don't live and speak the truth. *It's a matter of spiritual life and death.* John 10:10.

† Stick to the facts.

Often in a conflict, one person remembers one thing, but the other remembers events in a completely different way.

Our memories are subjective, and may not always be accurate.

The way you see something often has to do with the lies in your heart.

If you have a stronghold of rejection, for example, you may miss how your friend reached out to you and only see the ways she left you out.

So, if you say, "You don't care about me," you might be falsely accusing her. What if when you invited her to your house, she really wanted to go, but something prevented her?

It's best to just state the facts and take responsibility for your own feelings: "When I asked you to come to my house and you said no, I felt rejected."

† Don't mind-read.

If your friend tells you she has something else to do, just believe her. Don't imagine she's really just trying to get out of coming to your house because she doesn't like you.

Only God knows what someone's thoughts and motives are. James 4:12.

God didn't die and give you His job, so don't fool yourself into thinking you can read minds and judge motives. *Judging is a dangerous pastime.* See Matthew 7:1 and James 4:11-12.

If you really think there's something going on other than what your friend said, just ask her something like, "Is everything okay between us?"

† Own up to your messes.

If your friend answers that last question, "Well, the truth is you talk a lot about yourself, and sometimes I just want to know you care about me. That's why I don't come over anymore," how could you reply in a humble, Godly way? Matthew 5:23-26.
_____
_____

Everyone knows you're not perfect. It's no surprise. In fact, you look pretty silly when everyone can see your sin, but you deny it. Kind of like a little kid with chocolate all over her face saying, "Eat a candy bar? I would never do such a thing!"

If your friend approaches you about your sin, what should you do, according to Matthew 18:15?
_____

Read 1 John 1:8-10. When you deny your sin, whom do you call a liar? _____. Who is the real liar? _____.

Don't justify your sin or blame the other person for it. Memorize this sentence and use it often:

"I was wrong. Please forgive me."

✝ **Be transparent.**

What is the belt in your armor that helps you win the fight against the enemy? Ephesians 6:14. _____

As the Lord was teaching my friend about the importance of transparency, she had a dream one night. No matter where she hid, the enemy tracked her down. But when she became transparent, he couldn't find her to pick on her.

*Anything you hide in secret
the enemy can use against you.*

If you are in a battle, go first to the Lord, asking Him to help you. But also don't be afraid to talk with someone you trust who can pray with you and help you stand strong.

A friend who struggled with masturbation felt ashamed and embarrassed, but came to me for help anyway. We prayed together, asking God to topple the guardian lies of "I need it," "I can't help it," "Who's to know?" and "I'm not hurting anyone." That day, *Jesus set her free.*

Often, if you hold in a secret, the battle gets worse. But when you expose the enemy's scheme, the assault stops.

Make sure the person you share your struggle with is someone you can trust, like a mentor or a Godly friend. Let her ask you the hard questions and pray you through the times when temptation is fiercest.

✝ **Mean what you say.**

If you make a promise like "I'll always be there for you," then *BE there.* Don't lie just to make yourself or someone else feel good.

Don't say, "I'm so happy to see you!" when you're not. Get your heart right with God, and then *BE happy to see her.* Don't be fake.

At the same time, don't let your junk be an excuse to say ugly things. If you're angry, then ***there is usually a problem in you that you need to repent of.*** Matthew 5:21-22. Look for pride, selfishness, jealousy, or whatever sowed those anger seeds, and get your own mess cleaned up before you point out someone else's. Matthew 7:1-5.

✝ **Speak the truth in love.**

If you need to confront someone on a sin, *do it because you love her and want to see her set free,* not because you feel a need to lash out or protect yourself. Matthew 18:15.

Encourage others with the Word, (Ephesians 4:14-15) but have grace for them if they don't get it yet. 1 Corinthians 12:21-26. ***Live the truth, even if you're the only one doing it.***

Do you have any secrets the enemy is using against you? What are they? _____
_____

Whom can you trust to pray with you and help you fight? _____

Is there anyone you've hurt? A sin you need to repent of? Some way you haven't been honest? What do you need to do to get right with God and others?

_____
_____
_____
_____
_____

Check your own heart out first

Whenever you're in conflict, excuse yourself and get alone with God as soon as possible. Lay all your opinions of the other person down at His feet. Be real with Him. Tell Him, "I'm so mad at Susy because she...." Ask Him to show you any sin in your own heart. Repent. Then ask Him how HE sees her. Then when you speak to her, do so out of His love, not your own mess.

Delight in faithfulness — 34

Whom can I trust?

A best friend to me is one who is there for me. She laughs with me and shares the deep things of her heart. When I go through hard times, she listens, cares, and prays for me. She encourages me to grow in my walk with Christ. And when I'm under attack, she fights for me.

Do you have any friends like that? Who? _____

If you don't, ask God to give you some, and where He might want you to go to find them.

My friend Trish has been a rock in my life for many years. She has such a deep relationship with Jesus that if I'm struggling with something, I can go to her and know she will pray for me and seek God's answer together with me for my problem.

She doesn't force me to do things that go against my conscience, but encourages me to do what God desires. She doesn't judge me, but understands me, and helps me out of my messes. She doesn't imagine lies about me and spout them off at me in false accusations, but listens to me and loves me as I am.

A faithful friend and sister in Christ is a precious treasure. Proverbs 17:17.

But as wonderful a friend as Trish is, *she is not God.* She can't be there for me every moment like He is. Try though she may, she won't understand my heart as He does. *He made me. He lives in my heart. It is His home, and He knows me better even than I know myself.*

If you look to people to fulfill God's role in your life, you'll be disappointed.

People are people. They have junk in their hearts and make mistakes—even my dear friend Trish—because ... **Hurt people hurt people.**

Has a friend ever hurt you? Explain. _____

How did you feel when that happened? _____

Did you try to restore the relationship? How? _____

Did it work? Explain. _____

One of my deep, close friends once said to me, "If anything ever happens between us, I want you to know I'm here for you. We'll talk it out together until it's resolved."

But not long after that promise, she slipped into depression and stopped praying and worshiping. Her fun, chatty talk turned to passing judgment constantly on others, including me.

I tried to encourage her to lay her opinions at Jesus' feet so His truth could set her free, but she cut me out of her life. No talking it out. No telling me what I did that offended her. It was just over.

She had loved the Lord and been a good friend. We had shared secrets and walked through hard times together. We had ministered together, and our unity was sweet. She promised she wouldn't let anything separate us. But in the end, she broke that promise. She also left her marriage and church.

When I did a Word Search on "trust," guess what I found? Hundreds of verses say, *"Trust in the Lord,"* and only a handful say, *"Don't trust in men," "Don't trust in armies...."*

I realized the truth then, and it set me free from betrayal's pain: **I don't have to trust people. Or not trust them. *I just trust Jesus*. Period.**

When Jesus asked us to love God and love others (Matthew 22:37-40), He didn't say, *"if they love you back."* He just said, ***"Love."***

It's an unconditional command.

***Trust* Jesus, and *have grace* for your friends.**

Love your friends. Enjoy them. Forgive them. Speak truth to them. Be there for them as best you can. Ask forgiveness when you mess up. Be a faithful friend, even if they can't. And walk in the freedom of knowing Jesus is more than enough to satisfy all your needs to be loved.

- † He is always there for you.
- † He fights for you.
- † He understands you.
- † He accepts you as you are.
- † He challenges you to grow.
- † He always speaks the truth.
- † He wants what's best for you.
- † He is for you.
- † He speaks your love language.
- † He will never leave you or betray you.
- † He won't take you for granted.
- † He is good. In fact, He is *perfect*.
- † He can't sin against you, because He can't sin!
- † He listens, and cares.
- † He picks you up when you fall.
- † He comforts you.
- † He has grace for you and forgives you.
- † If you walk away from Him, He will pursue you with His undying love.
- † He pulls you out of a tight spot.
- † He laughs with you, cries with you.
- † He is a refuge in the storm.
- † He is a mighty warrior, a "friend in high places" no enemy can defeat.
- † He lavishes His love on you.
- † He honors you, treasures you.
- † He loves you too much to give you all you want; *He gives what you need.*
- † He gives you strength to keep on going no matter how hard things get.
- † His "pep talks" are the best!
- † He loves you unconditionally.
- † He knows your heart. He sees you.
- † He is faithful.

Jesus wants to be your best friend.

He carries no "baggage," because *He is holy.* He can't lie, falsely accuse or break a promise, because *He is Truth.* He can't run away from God and turn on you, because *He IS God.*

Do something special with Jesus today, something you might do with a best friend. (See some ideas below.) Talk with Him and listen for His voice all day. Don't worry if you don't hear Him right away. Just know He's listening and enjoy being with Him.

In your quiet time, pray through the bulleted list in this chapter, asking God to show you specifically how He has done those things for you. Write a prayer thanking Him for the ways He has been there for you. Now pray again through the list, asking Him to help you be a Godly friend to others.

_____
_____
_____
_____
_____
_____
_____

Dates with your Best Friend

Jesus wants to be your Best Friend. No matter what happens throughout the day, He's with you. So, when you're happy, tell Him about it. When you're sad, go to Him for comfort. Go for a walk with Him in the park. Take Him shopping. Ask Him for His opinions. Tell Him what you like and why. What matters to you matters to Him. He wants to be included in every part of your life and LOVES being with you. When HE fills the Best Friend place in your heart, you'll find you're a better best friend to others.

Delight in understanding

Overcoming conflict

Have you ever misunderstood someone? Explain. _____
_____
_____

Misunderstandings are common in friendships, in families, and even among strangers.

If you say, "The sky is blue" to five people, you could get five different reactions:

1. "She's right. It's really blue."
2. "It's not blue. It's purplish."
3. "Does she think we're so stupid we don't know what color the sky is?"
4. "Why did she change the subject?"
5. "What she's saying is she's sad today."

A true friend truly listens and joins you where you are. She may not fully understand what you're going through, but she cares.

No one has experienced what you have in life, so no one's thoughts are exactly like yours. But when your friend is hurting or angry or even happy, if you can set aside your own thoughts to truly listen to her and care about her feelings, she will have a true friend indeed.

Sometimes that's difficult to do, especially if your friend is angry at you. You may want to defend yourself or fight back.

But try *listening*. James 1:19, Matthew 18:15. Search your heart before the Lord as she speaks. If you really have done something hurtful, *apologize and try to change.*

> **Let everything you do be done in love.**
> 1 Corinthians 16:14.

I'm so grateful to friends who are honest with me, even if it hurts, because I don't always see what I'm doing wrong.

But often, people accuse, not because something's wrong with you, *but because something's wrong in their own hearts.*

Reasons Why People Attack:

- **Current crises.** If your friend is going through a hard time, the stress might push her to lash out at you, even if you're not involved.
- **Unhealed wounds.** Your actions, even if done in love, might have triggered a reaction from your fragile friend because something in her past or in a relationship with someone else is not yet forgiven or healed.
- **Guilt.** It's common for people to accuse you of something they themselves feel guilty for.
- **Justification.** If your friend is engaging in a sin you are not, she may accuse you of being "judgmental," or try to loudly reason away her actions, rather than repent.
- **Blame.** Some people avoid their own sin by pointing a finger at others: "Well, *you*..."
- **Mind-reading.** If your friend grew up in a dysfunctional family environment, she may have a habit of "reading between the lines" of what people say as a means of protecting herself. Even if you speak straight up, she could imagine you mean something else and respond adversely.
- **Strongholds.** People who walk in fear of judgment often judge you for judging them, even if you're not. And those who walk in pride or self-defense might imagine everything you say is about them, even when it's not. Every stronghold has a damaging effect on relationships. *We all need Jesus to set us free!*

This list is so compelling that I hope it moves you to compassion—to love your friend in her fragile, human state, and have grace for her.

Peace-provoking responses (Proverbs 15:1)

when attacked with false accusations:

† Try **saying back to her what she said to you:** "I hear you saying...." This lets her know you're listening and you care.

† If there is any truth to what she's saying, **ask her forgiveness.** Even if you didn't say what she said you did, you can still say, "Please forgive me for any way I hurt you."

† Ask her questions, like, "What made you feel that way?" This **helps her process her feelings,** so she can begin understanding what's truly going on in her heart. Once she can see the lies in there, then she might be willing to invite God's truth to tear them down.

† Offer to **pray with her.** When you pray for her, you are fighting for her against the enemy, asking God to heal her, help her, deliver her. If she's willing, walk her through the Galatians 5:22-23 Gauge. If the problem is in her heart, then it's not going away until she has an intimate encounter with Jesus.

People are people, and even the best of friends can be mean and hurtful at times. But God's love is the one sure thing I can always trust in. Romans 8:35-39. And it is only through His boundless love that I can step over others' junk—or even my own—to love as He first loved me. 1 Peter 4:8.

Don't be controlled by someone else's actions or words; be controlled by Love.

Think about a spray can. Add a little pressure, and what comes out? Whatever's in the can!

I want to be so full of Love, that when others "press my buttons," all that comes out is Jesus.

But that's hard, isn't it? How do you stay linked up to Love such that He flows through you even in the heat of an argument?

How to stay centered in Christ, even in the midst of conflict:

1. **Let Jesus be your First Love.** Let Him be your first thought in every situation all the time.

2. **Cleanse your heart so God's love controls you rather than the issues you haven't dealt with yet.** (See the Gauge in Chapter 16.)

3. **Look for Him in the moment.** Rather than busying your mind with a rebuttal to your friend's comment, ask God to show you what He's doing and to speak through you to her.

4. **Take responsibility for your own part in the conflict.** As long as your mindset is "I'm right and you're wrong!" you won't be able to hear or understand your friend. And you'll miss what God wants to do in you.

5. **Remember, you have an enemy, but it's not your brother or sister.** Don't fight against each other. Instead, fight *for* each other *against the real enemy.* 1 Peter 5:8-11.

6. **Intercede.** If your friend is fighting against you, unable to accept your love and forgiveness, then there are deep strongholds at work in her life. *Ask God to set her free.*

Cunning words or tight fists might win a human fight, but you've lost the real battle if you haven't responded God's way—*in love.* Romans 13:8-10.

Are you in a conflict? Position yourself to let God's love flow through you. Ask Him to clean out all the "residue" bad experiences have left in your "cup," and fill you with Himself.

Set aside your thoughts, feelings, and agendas to ask God how He sees the person and situation. Write out James 1:19 and tape it up on your mirror. Then purpose to use that strategy in conversation next time you're with her. What does Romans 12:9-21 say we should do to those who act against us? _____

_____

Listen first, speak later

*Jesus didn't turn the tables over in a flash of anger. He went to the temple, saw what was going on, spent time with the Father, slept, and **then went back the next day** to clean out the temple under God's leading. Mark 11:11-17. In the same way, it's good to take a step back before you respond in anger. Let God show you His perspective.* **Seek to listen more than to be heard, to understand more than to be understood.**

Delight in forgiveness   36

A yank-ee no longer!

One of the things that still blows my mind about Jesus is His forgiveness. It doesn't matter how far I fall, He always reaches out to pull me back up into His arms.

Now I can love because *His love empowers me.* I can forgive because *He has wiped my own slate clean.*

What are some opposites of the fruit of the Spirit in Galatians 5:22-25 that might come from unforgiveness? _____
_____

Did you know that unforgiveness is a leading cause of depression? If you let the sun go down on your anger (Ephesians 4:26), bitterness takes root and grows all kinds weeds.... But most depressed patients have left unforgiveness untended so long, *they don't even know it's eating away their life.*

Unforgiveness gives Satan a dangerous foothold.
Ephesians 4:26-27; 2 Corinthians 2:9-11

The truth is most offenders don't know they've hurt you. You might think you're punishing that awful person by not forgiving her, but most likely, she's oblivious, both to the offense and to your unforgiveness. *You* are the one who is "punished" when you don't forgive.

Forgiveness means cutting the strings that attach your heart to an offense, so Satan can't "yank" you around by it anymore.

In unforgiveness, you cut that person off from love and grace. But with forgiveness, you cut *yourself* free from the control that sin had on your heart.

In some circumstances, because of constant abuse by an offender with an unrepentant heart, God may ask you to separate yourself from the abuser. *This does not go against love or forgiveness.*

Forgiveness is not saying someone's sin is okay. Sin is never okay, especially sin that hurts others.

Forgiveness is
- † **Releasing my heart from the offense** that keeps it in pain.
- † **Releasing that person into the hands of God** to be dealt with by Him, for only He is Judge.

What do Mark 11:25-26 and Luke 6:37 tell us will happen to us if we don't forgive? _____
_____

That's pretty serious. Would you take such a risk just to hold a grudge?

Forgiveness is a choice before it is an emotion.

You may not *feel* like forgiving that person that did that horrible thing to you, but you can still *choose* to forgive.

Has someone's offense ever played over and over in your mind? Explain. _____
_____

When that happens, the enemy is prompting you because he wants to perpetuate anger, pain, bitterness, hatred, etc.

But you can strike back a deadly blow by *using the enemy's "prompting" as a reminder to fight for your friend.*

Striking back at Satan:
1. **Forgive the person who hurt you.** *"Jesus, I forgive Susy for saying those ugly things behind my back."*
2. **Bless her.** *"And I bless Susy in Jesus' name. Show me what I can do today to help Susy feel forgiven and loved, Lord."*
3. **Pray for her.** *"Draw Susy closer to Yourself, Lord. Take away her need to tear down others. I know her father's gone a lot and her mother's busy. Open up time in their schedules to spend with her so she can feel loved and secure. And in the midst of whatever pain she's feeling, be her Friend, Lord. Give her a hunger for You and let her know You are*

more than enough to satisfy all her needs."

4. **Intercede, asking for God's mercy for her.** *"Lord, the Word says those who judge will be judged. Matthew 7:1. So I ask You now to have mercy on Susy. Please forgive her, Lord, because she doesn't understand what she's doing. Luke 23:34. Give her a chance to repent and be reconciled to You. Set her free from judgment, gossip, low self-esteem, pride, and anything else that blocks her from the abundant life You give her in Christ."*

Why do you think prayers like these are such deadly blows to the enemy? _____
_____
_____

Prayer is powerful. Not only will the enemy fail to conquer you with anger and bitterness when you forgive, but *God just might set Susy free from the enemy's hold on her as well!*

In fact, if you respond this way in a conflict—by **praying for your offender every time the enemy tries to remind you of the offense**—the enemy loses more ground by reminding you of her evil deeds than if he leaves you alone. As a result, *he just might quit!*

Again, there is no excuse for sin. But two wrongs don't make a right. Susy may have sinned terribly against you, but *your sin is no better than hers if you don't forgive her.*

When you forgive, you are set free to find peace and rest in the arms of the only One vengeance belongs to—the One Who does you no wrong, Whose plans for you are good, and Who loves you with a perfect love. Romans 12:19.

Ask God to show you anyone you haven't forgiven. Hand your feelings about that person over to God, laying them at His feet.

Ask Him how He sees him/her, and write what He shows you. _____
_____
_____

Will you choose now to forgive, even if you don't "feel" like it? Walk through steps 1-4 and write your prayers here:

1. _____
_____

2. _____
_____

3. _____
_____

4. _____
_____

Ask God to defeat the enemy's schemes, and to restore the relationship if possible. Each time the offense returns to your mind, use it as a reminder. Walk back through steps 1-4 until the painful thoughts have stopped and you're free.

Freedom through forgiveness

When you feel the pain of an offense, even if it happened a long time ago, get alone with the Lord as soon as you can. Don't stifle your feelings or excuse away the person's sin, just pour out your heart to the Lord. Tell Him what happened and just how that made you feel. Then, in the midst of your pain and anger, speak out, "I forgive (person's name) for (offense done). And I bless her (him) in Jesus' name."

Delight in your King's choice

37

Princess in waiting

What are some qualities of Godly men in 1 Timothy 2:8; 3:1-12; 6:11; 2 Timothy 2:10, 16-17; 4:2, 5; Titus 1:6-9; 2:6-8? What other qualities have you observed that you like in Godly men you know?_____
_____
_____

A man of God loves God first. His actions and words are an outflow of that love. Matthew 22:37-40.

It's good to know what a Godly husband is like so you know what you're looking for. One of my friends even listed ten pages of qualities she wanted in a man; and *God actually answered every one of them.* My own list was much shorter:

1. That he love God first
2. Love me second
3. And love to worship

My husband is all that, plus tall, handsome, kind, gentle, fun to be with, and a great dad. The Lord answered my prayer and then some.

But some men that look like princes turn out to be toads; and others you pass over could be a prince in disguise. So, how do you know when you've met "the one"?

Read Genesis 24. Isaac lived in a land void of Godly women. Have you ever thought, "If only I went to another school, or lived in a different place...."? Do you feel sometimes like there's no one suitable around for you to even think about liking, much less marrying? Explain.

_____
_____

How can you have faith that God will provide? See Proverbs 21:1 and Psalm 31:15.

_____
_____

Several Christians I know who have said, "I feel called to missions, but I'm not going until I'm married," are now in their fifties still waiting for that magical spouse to appear.

But others who obeyed God's call, stepping into the darkest corners of the earth where there were no "eligible Christian singles," found that *God brought their husbands to them—not just any men, but Godly men with the same heart for Jesus and for the nations.*

Isaac looked up from his quiet time to see lovely Rebekah, God's answer to his prayers, slipping off her camel, exclaiming, *"Who is that man?"*

Were their hearts beating fast? Probably. Was it love at first sight? You bet! Genesis 24:62-67.

Your story will be different, of course. But the concepts in Genesis 24 remain the same:

1. Be a Godly woman. (v 16)
2. Pray for God's plan. (vv 12-15)
3. Walk closely with God, and He will not let you miss His perfect will for you. (v 40)
4. Submit to God's leading. (vv 50-51, 57-58)
5. Worship Him. (vv 26-27)
6. Love. (vv 62-67)

But what if God's will is for you to be single? Will you be okay with that? Why or why not?

_____
_____

Don't forget you're already betrothed. *The King who loves you beyond measure is the only One who can fill all the longings of your heart.* (Chapters 3-4)

So if you're thinking, "If only I were married, my life would be so much better," *your heart is headed for dangerous places.*

No man, no matter how wonderful he is, will fill up the lonely places of your heart. Only Jesus can.

So *use this time before you are married to fall in*

love with Jesus. Then if He brings you a wonderful husband who loves Him and loves you, that man will be blessed beyond measure, because *the pressure's off. He doesn't have to meet all your needs and be God for you.* You can just love him as he is—bumps and all.

What does Paul say is an advantage to being single? See 1 Corinthians 7:1, 8, 17, 25-35.

It is better to not be married than to marry the wrong man.

When I was single, God called me to Africa for three months, and off I went. When a friend needed help, I could drop everything and spend as much time with her as she needed.

In fact, I told the Lord I didn't want to get married unless I could serve Him better that way.

Then one day, I was strolling down the street with the man who is now my husband. I turned to speak to a beggar, but when the man said something uncomfortable, my husband answered him, and used the opportunity to share Jesus with him.

I would never have finished that conversation, and he would never have started it. Between that experience and several others, I realized God was saying: "See? Married to this amazing man, you can serve Me better!"

We did get married, and I love being his wife! Marriage is not without its hard knocks, of course. But then again, neither is being single. *So just enjoy Jesus, whatever state you're in.*

Have you come to the place yet in your walk with the Lord where He is the Lover of your soul, your Husband, the One who fills all your empty spaces? Explain. ___

If that still seems strange to you, study through Psalm 45; Isaiah 54, 61, and 62; Jeremiah 2:2, 32 and 3:14a; Hosea 2:16; 2 Corinthians 11:2; Ephesians 5:22-32. Now read Song of Songs, keeping in mind you are the bride of the King of Kings. Ask Jesus to pour His love over you. Write what He shows you. ___

Focus on the ever after

Don't spend time on self-pity, longing to be married when you're not. Instead, fix your eyes on eternal things. Hebrews 12:1-2; 2 Corinthians 4:18. How you love your neighbor today is far more important than a ring on your finger. Likewise, whether or not you get married isn't as "eternal" a matter as how you treat your husband once you are married. So use this time now to draw close to God and love others well, and you will live happily forever after—whether single or married.

Delight in true love

A kiss worth waiting for

What qualities would you like in a husband? _____
_____
_____
_____

What do you think such a perfect husband is looking for in a wife? _____
_____
_____
_____

Do you have those qualities? Explain. _____
_____
_____
_____

What do you want out of marriage? _____
_____
_____
_____

People spend a lifetime looking for true love. Some even think they've found it, only to watch it slip through their fingers. How many divorces do you know about? Or friends who have bounced from one messed up relationship to another, seeking acceptance and love from men too immature emotionally and spiritually to give it.

People say, "You have to kiss a lot of toads before you find your prince." But the truth is

Kissing toads gives you warts.

Girls who date around rarely come out of the experience unscathed. Either her own heart breaks, or she breaks someone else's.

Those **emotional warts** are real. They affect your attitude toward men and choices you make the rest of your life. In fact, my man-of-God son who's looking for a Godly wife keeps meeting young Christian women so messed up from former relationships they're afraid to get close to a man.

It takes a real man of God walking in the Spirit and fruit #9 (Galatians 5:22-23) to honor both your heart and your purity. So, don't dive into a relationship just because the guy seems cute, you're having trouble with your own fruit #9, or everyone else has a boyfriend so you want one too.

You could end up giving away what belongs to your husband long before you meet him. And *that prince your King prepared for you could pass you by while you're messing around kissing toads.*

Then there are **lifetime warts**. One of my college friends got pregnant from her first sexual encounter ever, dropped out of school, gave up her dream to become a Christian singer, and married the not-so-princely guy. *Just a few minutes alone with him cost her the rest of her life!*

Even one "innocent" kiss can land you with an illness like herpes, that bubbles up in pussy lesions all over your beautiful face over and over the rest of your life.

Yet more ghastly diseases come from sexual intercourse. That man who's making such a fast move on you has probably been with several other women before, so you're making your bed in some dangerous places; not only because of the emotional and **physical** warts that toad will leave with you, but the **spiritual** ones, as well.

If what I've shared so far isn't enough to convince you to save your kisses and intimate touch for the prince your King has prepared for you, I hope His words will:

Read 1 Corinthians 6:12-19. What does verse 12 mean to you? _____
_____
_____
_____

What is your body's purpose in verse 13?
_____
_____

How is that different from unbelievers?
_____
_____

Read verses 14-19. Why is it wrong to allow your body to touch or be touched in intimate ways outside of marriage? _____
_____
_____

You are not yours to give away.

Read the allegory of Israel as God's bride in Ezekial 16:1-14. How does this mirror what your King has done for you? _____
_____
_____
_____
_____

You belong to Jesus. You are His. *The closer and purer you walk with Christ, letting His beauty shine through you, the more attractive you will be to that man of God looking for a Godly wife.*

Have you already given away a kiss and more to a toad? Do you feel so violated or impure a prince won't want you? Or even your King? Has sin, shame or fear taken you over so completely you're afraid you'll never be free?

Your Savior says to you now, "My beloved, my beautiful one, *you are still Mine.* There is no sin I cannot redeem you from. I am Almighty, All-Powerful, compassionate, and I *see* you.

"Redeemer is My name. I look at your heart, past all that sin, *and I see My signature there,* pressed into who you are: **'Mine.'**

"So let Me hold you now. Here in My everlasting arms where you are safe and beloved. Let Me be your Protector, your Shield, your strong arms that never let go.

"Let the kisses from My mouth, My Word, My love, be enough for you. Let Me *satisfy you* with My love. For I gave My life so you could be free. There is no greater love than this. And no man will fill the longing in your heart. But Me.

"You are My desire. *Let Me be yours.*

"I have a future planned for you greater than your wildest imaginations, fuller than your brightest dreams, sweeter than your deepest longing.

"Step into My love and let Me make you whole again. For *redeeming is My specialty.* Don't think you're too far gone to be restored. For nothing is impossible with Me. Rescuing and restoring is what I do. I look at your sin but a moment, *and then I wash it away with My grace.* That is how I call you perfect, spotless, without blemish, My perfect, spotless bride.

"I offer you freedom today. Will you take it?

"Or do you not believe it's possible? Do you think I don't know what it's like to be tempted? Or that I don't understand your thoughts and desires?

"I was a man in every way. I know. I see. I understand, My love. If you believe I don't, or that I'll never want you after what you've done, then you don't know My character.

"I am Love.

"And *Love covers over a multitude of sins.*

"So step into My love and **be free.**"

(Isaiah 54:5, Psalm 4:8, 33:20, 32:7, Deuteronomy 7:19; 33:12, 27, 29; 2 Samuel 22:31, John 15:13, Song of Songs 4:7, Hebrews 10:14, Romans 3:24, 5:2, 6:14, 1 John 4:16, 1 Peter 4:8.)

Live the dream of all dreams

Your enemy wants to tell you there is no prince waiting for you, that you're not good enough, pure enough, beautiful enough; that you must settle for a man who shows an interest in you, even if he's not a man of God. Don't listen to him. Wait for your King. He knows what is best for your life. He has something beautiful planned for you. He wants to satisfy you with His love and give to you an abundant life. But your enemy wants to kill, steal and destroy. Whose path will you choose? Choose life. John 10:10.

Delight in your Healer 39

Deep healing for deep wounds

What has your love life been like?
_____
_____
_____

That may not be a happy question for some women. If you have been molested or abused in some way, please *seek a Christian counselor who will pray with you and help you to healing.*

But even if you have not been abused, there may be some way a man has wounded you.

Please pray through the following list and check what applies. If a memory comes to mind, put a star by that or make a note in the margin.

- ☐ In general, when you think of men, what feelings and thoughts come to mind? _____
_____
- ☐ Have you loved someone who rejected you?
- ☐ Did your father or someone else close to you cheat on his wife? Was a boyfriend unfaithful to you in some way? Are you afraid of divorce?
- ☐ Was your father emotionally abusive, distant, manipulative, undependable, mentally unstable, alcoholic, drug addicted, violent, absent, or is there any other way in which he wounded your spirit or body?
- ☐ Were you ever touched inappropriately, like by a parent, sibling, baby sitter, neighbor, even another child? Have you been molested? Raped? Sexually abused?
- ☐ Have you ever felt you aren't beautiful enough for a man to want you? Do you struggle with eating disorders, such as bulimia, anorexia or obesity? Have you considered surgery to be more attractive or unattractive to men?
- ☐ Have you ever kissed a guy? Let him caress you? Exposed your body to him? Slept with him? Participated in other sexual acts?
- ☐ Have you ever followed through on a dare, game, or initiation into a sorority, club, cult or occult where your body was used?
- ☐ Have you been with a married man or felt attracted to one? Are you divorced?
- ☐ Have you ever felt unsafe around a man? Has a guy ever hugged you inappropriately? Made uncomfortable advances toward you?
- ☐ Have you day-dreamed or fantasized about sexual adventures? Is there a man you commonly fantasize about?
- ☐ Do you stimulate yourself to orgasm?
- ☐ Have you had sexual dreams?
- ☐ Have you been molested by a sexual spirit (usually while sleeping: succubus/incubus)?
- ☐ What novels, movies, magazines, etc., have made you fantasize or linger on sexual thoughts? If a sex scene comes on in a movie, do you watch it? Does your mind ever return to those scenes later?
- ☐ Do you often flirt with men? Do you wear tight, short, low or otherwise revealing or sexy clothing? Do you speak, walk, dance or sit in such a way as to attract a man's attention? Do you post sexy poses of yourself on social media?
- ☐ Have you ever received obscene phone calls or texts?
- ☐ Have you ever texted or talked dirty with a guy, or exchanged revealing photos or messages with a him?
- ☐ Have you ever hooked up with someone for the purpose of sexual gratification?
- ☐ Have men made inappropriate, lewd or mean remarks about you or your body?
- ☐ Have you been sexually harassed?
- ☐ Have men in public places tried to touch you, make a pass at you, get you to go with them? Have you been "flashed" by a man showing

you his private parts in public?
- ☐ Have you had an abortion?
- ☐ Have you had lesbian thoughts or dreams, or been in a lesbian relationship?
- ☐ Other _____

Look back through the checks and stars. Which of those memories or feelings is the strongest? Ask the Lord to lead you to the one He wants to heal now. Even if what has unsettled you is a dream or a movie, you can **use the Galatians 5:22-23 Gauge to seek the Healer for healing:**

1. Ask the Lord to show you anything He wants to show you or take you anywhere He wants to take you, whether to that memory or to another. **Ask Him where that reaction** (lust, fantasy, fear, abandonment, rejection, seduction, hopelessness, etc.) **first began in your life.**
2. Feel what you felt when that situaton happened. **Look for the lies,** like, "I'm trapped," "No man will ever love me," "I can't trust men," "Men only want one thing," etc.
3. Did you make any vows, like, "I'll never fall for another guy ever again"?
4. Stay in that memory, feeling what you felt, and **ask the Lord, "Show me where You were when that happened. What were You saying? What were You doing?"** Look around in your memory for Him. He may change it for you so you can see what He was doing, or He might remind you of a Scripture or speak truth to your heart some other way. *This is the truth that sets you free*, so stay as long as you need to in His presence.
5. Write in your journal what God showed you, and **run it through the Three-Fold Sieve** (Chapter 13) to confirm His voice. Post it where you'll see it every day, like the mirror.
6. Did you find any unholy vows in #3? **Cut those off now.** (See Chapter 18)
7. Is the sin or negative reaction generational? Ask the Lord. If so, walk through the steps in Chapter 19.
8. As God leads, **cut off any soul ties** to the person(s) in your event. (See the next chapter.)
9. Command (or ask Jesus to command) any **demons** (of seduction, fear, shame, lust, rejection, etc.) **to go** in the name of Jesus. **Forbid them** to bother you or your descendants again.
10. Ask Jesus to **shield you** from further attacks, **fill you with the holy opposite** (love, joy, peace, acceptance, etc.), and **help you walk out in truth** and freedom.

I added some steps here to what you did in Chapter 16, and God may lead you to other steps for healing as well. Take time in your quiet times to seek Him for healing for the other starred or checked memories/emotions. If the memory is particularly traumatic, you may want a counselor or other believer with you as you pray.

And *forgive yourself*, even as your Healer has forgiven you. Whatever you've felt, whatever you've done, *He can and will redeem, cleanse and restore you*, if you let Him.

If you're having trouble doing that, this might help: Ask Jesus to step back into that memory together with you again. This time, stand with Him, looking through His eyes at yourself, and following His lead. For instance, He may urge you to gather that little girl (your former self) up into your arms and say, "It's okay now. It's all over. I forgive you," or something else.

Spend time with the Lord now, soaking in His presence. Listen to worship music. Read the Word. Be still. Fall asleep in His arms. Whatever He's doing in this moment, do that with Him. Let Him give you peace after the storm.

Better wait than sorry

Our tendency as single women is to grow weary of waiting for God's choice for a spiritual leader husband. We're anxious we may never find a Godly man, have a boyfriend or get married. So we settle for less. If this describes you or if you've been involved in sexual sin, it's not too late. Get out of that messy relationship, even if you "love" him. Ask God's forgiveness and get back on track. No matter what you've done, He wants to offer you His grace, draw you back into His arms and spread out a new path of freedom for you.

Delight in freedom and purity 40

Sin's slippery slope

Some of those encounters you checked in the last chapter may have happened when you were too young to protect yourself, and the strongholds or addictions you face today may be a result of that abuse. The enemy doesn't play fair!

If you are a victim of sexual harassment or abuse, dear sister and daughter in Christ, please hear this: *The Lord your God is fighting for you, even now. He is angry, and the enemy and your abuser are in serious trouble!*

These Scriptures may be of blessing to you or someone you know who has been abused:

- Matthew 18:1-10
- Ezekial 16:4-14
- Isaiah 54
- Isaiah 51:21-52:3

As you walked through those steps with the Lord in the last chapter, I hope He met you in deep, healing ways.

But if you continue to struggle with a sin or thought, each time you feel yourself falling, *turn to the Lord* to help you. 2 Corinthians 10:3-5.

If you walk through the Galatians 5:22-23 Gauge for every negative thought or dream outside of the fruit of the Spirit, *you will be changed.* Romans 12:1-2, John 8:31-32, 36.

I know because the Lord has done that for me. I think the enemy must have placed a big red target on my head, because things that never happen to other women have been happening to me my whole life, and even seem "normal," like, "This is just what women have to go through as long as there are men in the world."

Is that thought familiar to you? Explain.

_____
_____
_____

You have a real enemy who is out to steal your purity, maim you with shame, and cuff you in chains to give in to his purposes rather than your King's.

Will you let the Mighty Warrior, your King, dash in with His sword ablaze and His eyes shining with love for you, and set you free? Isaiah 42:13. Or does that feel too impossible to be true?

Jesus did that for me. No matter what I've done or what's been done to me, He forgave me, healed me, transformed my thoughts, and freed me. Traumatic memories the enemy meant for permanent evil in my life and marriage no longer affect me. I am free! My marriage is sweet and fulfilling, and so is my walk with my King.

But I had to purpose to let Him set me free.

And not every stronghold is busted to pieces in five minutes. Some are. In fact, many of mine were. But others take much longer, because Your King wants to press His truth deep into your heart and rebuild your temple brick by brick into something beautiful and filled with His glory.

The Lord took me through several processes to set me free from strongholds, including the scriptures and steps discussed in this book. But you will need to lean into Him for the specific path to healing He has for you.

The journey is just as important as the destination.
You were created for intimacy with God, and drawing near to Him is the only way to draw near to Him. So *draw near now!* James 4:8.

Prayerfully read 1 Thessalonians 4:3-8. What is God's will for you?

1. (v. 3) _____
2. (v. 3) _____
3. (v. 4-5) _____

4. (v. 6) _____

5. (v. 7) _____

Why is it dangerous to reject these instructions? (v. 8) Whom are you rejecting? _____

Walking through the steps in this book will open the way for freedom. But to *live* free, *you must retrain your thought patterns.*

Write Romans 12:1-2 into a prayer from your heart to God's. _____

Jesus said **if your mind even dwells on an inappropriate thought, you've already committed the act.** Matthew 5:27-28. And Galatians 5:19-21 warns that **impurity and sexual immorality will steal your spiritual inheritance from you.** That's a high price to pay for temporary gratification!

Maybe you were standing strong, saving all your kisses and caresses for your husband. But then you gave in. Just once. And then again. And again. The more you willed yourself to stop, the more powerful the temptation grew. Romans 7:19. That's sin's slippery slope in James 1:13-15.

Something happens in the spiritual realm when we bind ourselves sexually to a man: the two become one. Matthew 19:5. It is a holy union meant for marriage. Beautiful. Sacred. Blessed. And a picture of Christ becoming one with His bride, the church. Ephesians 5:25-32.

But when we bind ourselves in thought or action with a man who is not our husband, we sin against that man, our husband-to-be, and the Lord Whose temple is our body.

Binding ourselves together as one with sin is dangerous. It opens the door to Satan to wreak havoc in our lives, that man's, our children's, etc.

1 Timothy 5:1-2 urges us to **treat men as our brothers with "all purity."** *This is your guide to Godly relationship.*

Take a moment to be still before the Lord and ask Him to bring to mind anyone you have not treated in "all purity" like a brother (or sister, if you've struggled with lesbian thoughts), whether in thought or deed; or anyone who has not treated you in all purity. Write the names down as they come to mind, then mark them out one-by-one as you walk through the next paragraph.

Because of 1 Corinthians 6:12-20, **cut off any physical, spiritual, mental, emotional, sexual, etc., ties** to those men (women). For example, *"Forgive me, Lord, for ... and for leading (name) into sin. In the name of Jesus, I cut off any unholy ties to (name), and release him to receive Your forgiveness and mercy and to have a blessed marriage founded on You...."* Spend time praying for him (her), and for your own marriage.

If your list is long, don't feel like you have to get through it in a day. Take your time, asking God to show you any way that person's junk has affected your life or yours has affected his (hers), and let Jesus cleanse, heal, cover, forgive, make you new.

Agree with God that sin is sin. Don't make excuses. Don't listen to what others say. *Know the Word. See sin the way God does. Hate it. And repent.*

Here's some ammunition to help blow down those prison walls: 1 Thessalonians 4:3-8, Colossians 3:5-9, Ephesians 5:1-17, Galatians 5:16-25, 1 Corinthians 6:9-20, 3:16-17, Romans 6:12-19, Hebrews 13:4-5, Matthew 5:27-28, James 4:7-8, 1:21-25, 2 Timothy 3:1-7, 2:20-22.

Forgive yourself

Your sin is no surprise to God. Long before you made the choice (or the choice was made for you) He already knew what you would face, and He already put His plan into motion for your rescue. So don't let shame and condemnation overwhelm you. That sin is already paid for. Forgive yourself as He has forgiven you.

Delight in turning the battle around

New mind, new habits

You were created for oneness, intimacy, love, acceptance, worth, belonging, power....

But **those holes are God-sized.** If you try to fill them with romance novels, movies, attention from men, or anything else, you'll come up empty.

The most powerful deterrent to temptation is a deep, vibrant relationship with God.

Whatever void you were trying to fill, *ask God to fill it with Himself.*

It's important to recognize Satan's lies, see his fingerprints on the attacks and temptations he tailor-makes for you, and **walk the opposite way.**

Read Proverbs 28:13 and James 5:16. What is God saying to you about secret sin?

_____

_____

Lust grows in isolation, secrecy and darkness.

Work hard to **stay away from alone situations with a man**, especially at night, and even if you think you're "just friends." He may not have the same idea!

Get in the habit of having others with you whenever you are with a man. If you find yourself alone with him, keep the door open, call a friend you trust and ask her to come, invite him to go with you someplace public....

Seek friendship with men, rather than an exclusive relationship that blocks out your friends, God and any thought but him.

Touch is a trigger that will drive you to want more, so guard against starting something that is soon to escalate.

Remember God is watching you. This is His precious son He loves and honors and wants to save in all purity for his wife. And He also wants to keep you pure for your husband. Ask Him to help you overcome your weakness and to show you the "way of escape" every time you are tempted. 1 Corinthians 10:13.

Don't assume that just because a man loves God he doesn't have a lust issue. And don't assume that just because you don't have sexual thoughts toward your friend, he doesn't toward you.

With easy accessibility to pornography and the degradation of moral values today, you need to assume that most men you meet have seen pornography or participated in sexual acts in some way, no matter how "pure" they seem.

There are some glorious exceptions to that rule, and I pray your husband is one of them, but you need to assume that if you date or are alone with a man, he may pressure you into more than you planned to give away. Or maybe *you* are the one you don't trust. Either way, **hang out with men together in groups with other friends**.

And pray for your husband-to-be and the other men you know, that God will set them free (because He most certainly can!) and keep them pure and set apart, both unto their King and unto the woman they will marry.

In fact, give your guy friends *Dare to Be a Man of God,* or suggest that study to your youth or singles minister to use with men in your church. (See www.MoreThanAConquerorBooks.com.)

You are not yours to give away, and neither is that son of the King you're attracted to, until the day your Heavenly Father gives His consent and you are married. 1 Corinthians 6:12-20.

Also, **strongholds go both ways**. If you experience an overwhelming draw to a man, *he might have a sexual stronghold and the demons assigned to draw women to the thought of him could be tugging at you.* Ephesians 6:12.

Try saying under your breath, **"If this is the enemy, stop it in the name of Jesus."** Then pray

for that man's freedom, salvation or however else God leads. I've used this warfare tactic many times and *it really works!* The battle disappears within seconds because I'm fighting for that man's purity, and *the enemy loses more ground by trying to attract me to him than if he had left me alone.*

If you struggle with fantasies or self-stimulation, then *set up a way of escape.* Eliminate isolation. Have a Godly female friend on speed-dial you can call to pray for you or come hang out with you. Fill your evenings with worship, Bible study, friends who love God.

Fix your eyes on the Lord, worship Him only. If your mind begins to wander, don't just think you can will yourself to stop. Your willpower isn't enough to break free from your prison. *You need Someone stronger.* So worship God. Hand your thoughts to Him. 2 Corinthians 10:3-5. Go back through the Galatians 5:22-23 Gauge and *turn the battle around.*

Ask God to lead you to a counselor, mentor or accountability partner who will ask you the hard questions, pray for you and with you regularly and help you draw closer to the Lord.

Also, **pray cleansing prayers through your home**, especially your bedroom, asking God to send out anything unclean and to fill your home with His presence and angels. Deuteronomy 7. Declare each room holy unto the Lord and cancel any rights the enemy might feel he has to bother you because of acts done by you or former tenants. Pray special blessings over your bed, asking God to protect your dreams and fill them with Himself. Play worship music throughout your home day and night, and sing along. Put scriptures up, and anything else God shows you to do to keep your home "clean" and your mind focused on Him.

Take 1 Timothy 5:1-2 seriously. If you really love your brother you'll *fight for his purity.* The opinion, "I should be able to wear whatever I want. It's the *man* that needs to get his thought-life under control," is not loving.

When he's at church to worship God, but you wear that tight, short, spaghetti-strap dress and then stand right in front of him, *you're asking him to look at you, not God.* Because of Matthew 22:37-40 and so many other passages, that just won't make it through the Three-Fold Sieve!

Men are triggered to lust by what they see, and women are turned on by a man's attention. You can see how that is a dangerous combination. We wear sexy clothes because they make us feel beautiful and we get extra attention from men. But *we have no idea what we're really doing to them.*

The way we dress, speak and act can *lead a man to sinful thoughts,* even when he never planned to think that way. Matthew 5:27-28.

I don't know about you, but *I don't want to be used by Satan to make someone sin.* Read Luke 17:1-2, what did Jesus say about leading someone to sin? _____

_____

Men I surveyed said these are common lust-triggers for them:

- **Breasts and cleavage.** Fashions today rarely cover your breasts, and tank tops move about, especially when you bend over. So I cut and sew a tank top into my bra high enough to cover me even when I bend over.
- **Bare shoulders, back.** Spaghetti straps or no straps are the most dangerous.
- **Slitted skirt.** That leg peeking through!
- **Skin.** Belly, hips, shoulders, thighs. Stay away from short or low shorts, skirts, tops.
- **Panties or bra showing.**
- **Skin-tight or see-through.**

When you go shopping, ask the Lord to lead you to just the clothes He has for you. If you're not sure about an outfit, ask your father, brother or Godly guy friend. *You can look stunningly beautiful without showing the world what only your husband should see and desire.*

Love your brothers

Look at every man as a brother or father. Treat him with dignity, respect and absolute purity, as Jesus would. If you truly love him, you'll fight for his purity. 1 Timothy 5:1-2. The husband God gives you will be a precious treasure. Guard your kisses and yourself for him. He's looking for a Godly wife, too.

Delight in Kingdom Culture dating

Path to solid ground

When a team of prayer walkers came from a mountainous country to hike with us into areas where no one had heard Jesus' name, rains ravaged the land with flash floods, making for a perilous path of new rivers and waterfalls. At one point a landslide had taken down the side of the mountain, leaving a slippery slope of mud in its wake. One misstep would have sent us to our deaths in the raging river hundreds of feet below.

But Angel (that was really his name!), an expert hiker, said to me, "Grab my hand and step only where I step." He strode out into the deep mud, leaving footprints for me, set and safe, so I wouldn't sink.

But I was afraid, and at one point I saw what seemed to me a better path, so I took a step out, and Angel said, "No! Step only where I step!" His strong arm pulled me back into his footprints and led me to solid ground.

How is what Angel did for me that day a picture of what Jesus wants to do for you? Psalm 40:2.

_____
_____
_____

Whatever you've been in the past, choose now to be that woman of God He created you to be. Take your King's hand, step into His footprints and let Him lead you out of whatever muck you're in.

There's nothing more appealing to a man of God than a woman on fire for Christ.

Guidelines to find the one God has for you:

1. **Walk close to your King.** In this life, you will face many dangers, and some of those may involve the men you know. You're not stuck. You don't have to go through with the path you're on. Your Savior is offering you the way out. Grab His hand, step where He steps, and let Him lead you to a spacious place where you can breathe again.

2. **Love Jesus first.** Matthew 6:33. You are on a journey to draw closer to the One you love. He may bring to you an earthly husband, as well. But this life here on earth is about loving God, feeling His great love for you, and loving others through His love. Matthew 22:37-40. Walking as one with the Lord is the only path to true joy. If you don't know how to get back on track with Him, start with daily quiet times, even when you don't feel like it. Ask God to give you a yearning to be with Him. Then look back through this book, putting into practice the suggestions in each chapter.

3. **Let the King arrange your marriage.** Your Heavenly Father loves you even more than you love yourself, and the man He has picked out for you will be a treasure beyond measure. Make your mission not about finding an earthly husband but about being a faithful bride to your Heavenly One, and when it's time for Him to bring that Godly man into your life, *his bride will be ready!*

4. **Act like a daughter of the King.** Love the men around you as brothers in all purity. 1 Timothy 5:1-2. Don't lead them to sin by the way you dress or act. 1 Timothy 2:9-10, Matthew 5:27-28. Be a loving sister to them, and most of all, love your King. Because it is His Spirit within you that a man of God will be drawn to.

5. **Don't go out with someone you wouldn't marry.** In most cultures, if a boy asks you out, he plans on kissing you and a lot more, *even if you've only just met*. But you are a princess and your culture is Kingdom Culture. You're not here to gratify men's lusty fantasies. You

are betrothed to the King of Kings. So, work out with the Lord an answer for when a guy asks you out that you don't know well enough to know he's the one. And don't fall into the trap of thinking you can change a man or rescue him if you date him. That relationship will only bring you and your children a lot of heartache. *Rescuing is Jesus' job*, not yours.

6. **Don't jump into romance. Be friends first.** It takes a lot of situations to truly know someone. If you jump straight into a dating relationship with a toad who dresses like a prince, saying the "right" things to make you think he's Godly, you could be headed for disaster. *Get to know him* first before you go out with him. Watch how he acts in different situations. Marriage is for life, so you want that person to be your best friend anyway, don't you?

   - How does he treat his parents, siblings, friends, those who oppose him?
   - Is passion for Christ evident in his lifestyle? Does he lead out in spiritual matters? Worship? Pray? Study the Word? Obey? Love others? Have grace for them? Help those in need? Serve?
   - Is he lazy? Argumentative? Selfish? Critical? Proud? How does he handle money?
   - What does he want to do with his life, and does that agree with what you feel God is leading you to do?

7. **Let your friends know your intentions.** If everyone knows you don't just date to date, but that you're looking for a man of God and you want to know him well before you go out with him, that will weed out a few toads and make a prince desire you all the more.

8. **At last, when you feel a peace that this is the one God has for you, date with the purpose of marriage.** Make Jesus the center of your relationship. Pray together, study the Word together, seek the Lord together for things He wants you to do as a "team." And remember only Jesus can fill those empty spaces in your heart. So set that man free to not be God, and God to be your Husband.

Your King says to you now, "Love Me, My beloved, above everything else, and I will give you the joy you seek. I will press out every tear into the palm of My hand and replace them in your eyes with tears of joy.

"I will satisfy your every longing, fill you with My Spirit and empower you to do what you never thought imaginable. I will secure your future to be exactly what you were created for, the perfect fit just for you, and you will know *this is what you were always destined for ... for I am the One you've been destined for.*

"Wherever you go, there I will go with you and there I will already be. And you will shine bright as the stars at night as you love through My love and see through My eyes. I will withhold nothing from you, for you are Mine, and I am yours. Forever.

"But step off my path and you could get stuck in a slide into a turbulent future.

"Yet even if you do, My love, I will be there to pick you up and help you to stand. For you were made for *My* love. And My love never fails. I will follow you whatever path you take and be there for you when you weep. I will pull you up into My mighty arms of love and hold you, restore you, love you.

"So do not be afraid. Seek Me and you will find Me. Love Me first and you will not miss the love I place in your path for you to love through My love."

Meditate on Psalm 73:25, and write a prayer to the Lord from your heart here. _____
_____
_____
_____
_____

Passion for Christ is the key

In your heart are empty spaces only Jesus is meant to fill. If you think, "If only I had a boyfriend or husband...," you're just headed for the pain of unquenched longing. Even the most wonderful man in the world falls short! So find that place of intimacy with Christ as your Husband (Hosea 2:16); and then if you do get married, His love will make your marriage all the sweeter.

Delight in glorifying God   43

Want to be a star?

You are in a race. You haven't arrived at the finish line yet. But every step of faith draws you closer—closer to the One you love, the One you will spend all of eternity with.

Run to win the prize! Hebrews 12:1-3.

Many of the lessons in this book I only just learned. Others took me months, even years, to truly understand and "run" in. But I've shared them with you now, while you're young, so you can know early on the Truth that sets you free. Proverbs 4:11-12.

If ever you trip or fall, don't give up. Let Jesus heal your wounds and pick you up, so you can run all the faster toward Him.

Remember, there is no sin so vile, no pit so deep, no prison wall so thick that He can't rescue you. *Saving, after all, is His business.*

So, open your heart to Him, let Him save you from your messes, and even make something beautiful out of them.

He loves you, and His one desire is that you feel His love, enjoy Him, love Him back, and shine His light to others around you.

Read 2 Corinthians 4. What are unbelievers blind to? (v. 4) Who has blinded them? _____

_____

You have a treasure beyond measure. (v. 7) What is it? What does that treasure enable you to do? _____

_____

Don't hoard your treasure!

All around you lost people are dying without Christ. God has placed you in their path for a reason—to shine His light to them!

Read Daniel 12:3, Isaiah 58:6-14, and Genesis 15:1-6. Keep your Bible open as we study.

In Daniel 12:3 what does God want us to do with others? _____

_____

What are some ways we can do that, according to Isaiah 58:6-14? _____

_____

"Honor Him, not doing your own ways, nor finding your own pleasure, nor speaking your own words. Then you shall delight yourself in the Lord."
Isaiah 58:13b

Write in your own words the three ways to honor God mentioned in the above verse.

1. _____
2. _____
3. _____

How could you walk these out in specific situations in your life? _____

_____

And in that same verse, what is your reward? _____

_____

How does that compare to Genesis 15:1? _____

_____

Will we be protected as we step out to obey

God? How? See Isaiah 58:8b and Genesis 15:1. _____

In Genesis 15:6, what did Abraham gain by believing God? _____

In Isaiah 58:8, how is that intertwined with God's protection? _____

What other promises does God give us in Isaiah 58:6-14 when we shine His light to others? _____

What does Daniel 13:3 compare us to when we are wise and bring others to righteousness? _____

Abraham was called to shine God's light to the nations. What did God compare his descendents to in Genesis 15:5? _____

That verse was a promise for you. Why? See Galatians 3:26-29. _____

Now read Philippians 2:14-16a. What are you like when you hold out God's Word to a dark world? _____

Isaiah 58:8a describes His light in you as the _____. What does that dispel as it breaks forth? _____

Can you see how God created you not only to know Him and love Him, but to draw others to Him as well, like moths to a flame?

Write Proverbs 4:18 in your own words as a prayer for yourself. _____

Who are some people in your life who don't know Jesus? What will you do this week to shine God's light to them? _____

Read Isaiah 61:1-3, and write it into a prayer, asking Jesus to shine through you. _____

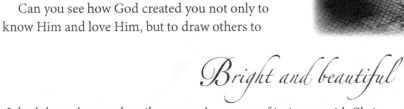

Bright and beautiful

I don't know how to describe to you the ecstasy of intimacy with Christ—of feeling His love and loving Him back, hearing His sweet voice and obeying, dancing through life with Him every moment. But it's what you were made for. Without it, life loses meaning. Don't close the lid on your treasure, and don't hoard it! . . .
SHINE!

Leader's guide for small groups

Is God leading you to gather several young women to study these life lessons from the Word together? Or are you a mother who would like to study *Delight to Be a Woman of God* with your daughter?

I'd love to journey together with you in prayer. Please feel free to write me at MoreThanAConquerorBooks@gmail.com with any questions.

"Lord, You Who created these beautiful young women to know You and to love You, please come and meet them now as they study Your Word. Open their eyes to see You as You truly are, to love You with all their hearts, and to run after You every day of their lives. Thank You for Your servant who will lead them in this study. Empower her, Lord, and flow Your love through her, so each woman she teaches feels the fullness of Your love. Ephesians 3:16-21. Be loud, O Lord. Let these women hear Your voice, feel Your touch, see You moving greatly in their lives. May they each know You as their Husband, Friend, Counselor, Guide, Strong Tower, Mighty Warrior, and Savior—their Life, their Love, their Song. Dance with them, Lord! In Your precious name. Amen."

I recommend you assign 1-2 Bible studies a week because of busy schedules and time needed to digest and walk out in the lessons they are learning. But you can do more or less as the Lord leads.

As young women sign up to come, advise them to bring their Bible, this book and a journal to the meetings. The "Delight to Be a Woman of God Prayer Journal" is available at www.MoreThanAConquerorBooks.com with or without lines and with special study helps for quiet times, but any notebook or journal will do. Encourage them to write in their journals every day, noting what God is teaching them in their quiet times and through life experiences. You keep one, too. It's an excellent way to commit God's words and lessons to memory and to life.

The smaller the group, the easier it is for everyone to participate. So, generally, groups of 4-8 make for the best discussions. But let the Lord lead you in this decision.

Everyone has different leadership styles. Feel free to ask the Lord how HE would want to lead these sessions. But for your information, here are some keys He's taught me:

† **Be accountable.**

If you don't already have a mentor, pray and ask God whom you can ask to cover you as you lead. This could be your spouse, a church staff member, or just a Godly friend. You need someone who will pray for you through questions and difficulties.

In addition to mentors, I often have a "right-hand" woman with me when I lead small groups—someone who will come early and pray with me in the room, then sit with us praying and participating throughout the meeting, then debrief with me afterward. If I get sick or can't lead for some reason, she can step in for me.

This can be another adult, or it can be one of the women in your group.

❧ **Enlist intercessors.**

Get church members, parents and other intercessors involved in praying for you and the women as you study and meet each week. But keep private things said in your meetings confidential.

You can ask the women if they know of people who would like to pray for them during this study.

❧ **Stay ahead.**

Do these lessons in your quiet times, but don't wait until the day before you lead. Study them a week or so early so you have several days to walk out in the truth yourself before you teach on it. The richness of your own experience will motivate those you lead to have a deep walk with the Lord.

❧ **Pray.**

The more you pray and surrender these studies and these young women into God's hands, the more powerfully He will move. Here are some great ways to pray for your group:

- † **As you prepare.** Ask God what He's doing, so you can come in line with Him and speak what's on His heart.
- † **In your quiet times**, for the young women in your study throughout the week.
- † **In the room before the meeting.** Get there 30 minutes or more early to ask God to fill the room with His presence and to move in the meeting. I like to touch each chair where people will sit and pray for God's special touch on each person.
- † **To start the meeting**, once everyone's gathered. Invite God to do whatever He wants. I like to open a meeting with worship too. Worship invites God's felt presence, and it will help everybody fix their eyes on Jesus, even before you dig into the Word. Don't worry if you're not musical. Some of the most incredible group worship times I've enjoyed have been with a music player and speakers. But make the words available for them, so they can participate.
- † **During the meeting silently**, even as you listen to others' questions or answers. Ask God to open their hearts and to give you wisdom. Keep looking for what He's doing, and follow Him there.
- † **Afterward** for God to seal in their hearts what He was saying to them, so they can walk out in what they've learned.

Begin with worship.

I suggest about 20-30 minutes of worship, as the Spirit leads, at the beginning of each meeting.

Give freedom to everyone to worship any way she feels comfortable. Some may sing, some may lift their hands, some may sit still, some may lie down, some may kneel, some may draw, and some may even sleep! Don't let anyone judge another for the way she worships, but let everyone feel comfortable.

You might want to intersperse spontaneous Scripture reading or prayer throughout the music or invite people to express verbally how great God is or read a psalm—however the Spirit leads.

Afterward, you might want to ask what they felt God saying during the worship time, before you move into the lesson study. This will encourage all of you to look for what God might be doing.

You can lead the worship time yourself, or enlist someone else to lead worship each week. It's wonderful to have live worship with instruments and such, and some of the young women in your group may play instruments and be willing to help in this. But audio-digital worship music is also an excellent option.

I suggest you ask the girls which worship songs touch their hearts, then keep a list (including the songs you enjoy Him with) to draw from to arrange worship.

How do you arrange a worship set?

- † For 30 minutes of worship, you're usually looking at about 6 songs.
- † Make sure you have the words to those songs available for each person.
- † Organizer-types might begin with praise songs about how wonderful God is, and then move into more intimate songs, such as about how much He loves us and we love Him. Or you can do it the other way around, too. But my favorite way to arrange a worship set is to pray, then listen to God. Whatever songs pop into my mind after dedicating that time to Him, I begin arranging how they feel like He's leading.
- † The best way to know how to lead others in worship is to worship in your own quiet times.

Expect God to show up.

Be looking for God during the sessions, so you can follow whichever direction He's leading. Don't worry if you don't cover the lesson or if you need to meet together again to discuss the same theme. It's not about getting something done; it's about drawing closer to Christ. Just let the Holy Spirit have full freedom to lead you in His directions. Most definitely plan for each session, but listen to God as you plan, and surrender the meetings over to His leadership.

Pray for each other.

Whenever someone shares from her heart or mentions something she feels God leading her to do, stop everything, gather around her, pray for her, and encourage her, reading any Scripture appropriate to the situation. Encourage them to call each other during the week to ask about each other and pray for each other.

⌘ Be transparent.

Be real with these young women, so they will feel free to be real with you. Share about mistakes you've made and how God grew you through them. If you don't understand something in the study and aren't sure how to walk out in it, feel free to say so, and ask the girls to pray for you during your time together that week. Then be prepared to share the next week how God answered, or how you are still working on it.

⌘ Keep confidentiality.

Whatever is shared in each session should stay within the group so that each person feels safe. If Veronica tells a story, no one should tell it outside the meeting, unless Veronica gives her permission.

Another key to helping the young women feel safe is to have a closed-door policy. Only those who are committed to come are allowed to come. No newcomers once the group has been established. But this needs to be discussed and prayed about together as a group. If, after the doors are closed, someone wishes to join, you should ask God about it together, because that person may be sent there by Him. So be flexible according to His leading.

⌘ The Word is your source.

If someone asks a question, don't just answer it off the top of your head. Make it an adventure to dig into the Word for the answer. If someone asks, "Is it okay to smoke?" for example, don't just say "No." Look up Scriptures in a concordance that deal with our bodies or on glorifying God, and assign the girls to prayerfully read those Scriptures during the week, asking the Lord to speak to them. Then come together the next week to see what God said. Or read the Scriptures there in the meeting together, praying and asking God to speak. This teaches them to go to God for the answers to all of life's questions.

⌘ Encourage discussion.

As you prepare, ask God to give you some good questions to ask from the lesson, or Scriptures for the girls to discuss.

Some people are more talkative than others are, so listen to the Lord as to how to draw the quiet ones out and rein the vocal ones in. You want everyone to participate, as He's doing different things in different people, and we all need each other to grow together in Him. Ephesians 4.

Here are some ideas for discussion questions:

† What was this chapter about? Summarize in your own words.
† What did you like about this chapter? Why?
† What did you feel God speaking to your heart about in this chapter?
† Is there anything God is asking you to do? A command to follow? A sin to confess?
† How do you plan to walk out in that?
† How are you doing with walking out in what we talked about last week?

Give the participants opportunities to lead.

The ones who lead are usually the ones who grow the most (that means you, too!), so ask God to direct you in assigning leadership tasks to different ones in your group—to lead in prayer or worship or even in some of the sessions. Have them take turns in these different tasks, so each one has a chance to develop and grow in different areas of leadership.

If you finish this study and want to do another, we recommend,

Dare to Become a Kingdom Culture Leader.

Find it now at
www.MoreThanAConquerorBooks.com.

You can also follow me on Twitter, Facebook, Pinterest and Wordpress.

Step into the adventure...

Mikaela Vincent
More Than A Conqueror Books

We're not just about books. We're about books that make a difference in the lives of those you care about.

www.MoreThanAConquerorBooks.com

Deepen the Delight

with these inspirational devotionals, Bible studies and novels by Mikaela Vincent. Find these books and more at

MoreThanAConquerorBooks.com

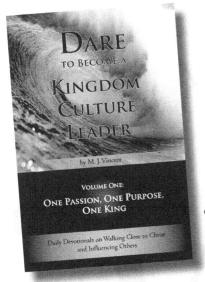

Dare to Become a Kingdom Culture Leader
Volume One: One Passion, One Purpose, One King
Volume Two: Oneness and the Watchman Warrior

Step into the destiny you were created for.
Become a Kingdom Culture Leader.

Most of us want to make a lasting difference here on earth. We don't want to just live and die and be forgotten. Not that we need to have some important name or anything. But we want our lives to count for something. Something that matters. Something that lasts and influences others in such a way that this world is a little brighter, a little better because we lived.

Whether you're a parent, teacher, pastor, missionary, leader, or even just Joe Blow Christian, this book of daily devotions and Bible studies is for you.

Through practical lessons on listening to God's voice, making wise decisions, following the Spirit's leading, walking in humility, promoting unity, and leading others well, Vincent digs into the Word to form new thought processes and habits so we can keep in step with the King of Kings and lead out as Kingdom Culture influencers.

Dare to Be a Man of God

Do you have a brother or a friend who might benefit from deep Bible study too? Dare to Be a Man of God is filled with Scripture and thought-provoking questions to help young men to freedom from strongholds, walking in the Spirit, remaining pure and finding the wife God has chosen for them. (Group study leader's guide included.)

Dare to Be a Man of God Prayer Journal

This quiet times companion to Dare to Be a Man of God is packed full of steps to listening to God's voice and walking as one with Him.

Bible Studies and Devotionals for Middle School & Teens

Delight to Become a Woman of God
30 Bible studies from a mother's heart to her daughter's on drawing near to Christ and loving well

It's not a fairy tale. It's true. You really are a princess, destined to marry the King. And together you'll live happily forever after. It's all you ever dreamed life could be, and it's all yours, if you choose to become a woman of God. This Bible study guide for young women ages 12 and above, offers original illustrations, personal stories, deep questions, and Scripture to point young women to deeper depths with Christ so they can be set free from the things that keep them from the abundant life they were created for. A group study leader's guide is included. But this workbook can also be used for personal quiet times.

Dare to Become a Man of God
30 Bible studies from a mother's heart to her son's on drawing near to Christ and living victoriously.

Whether you like it or not, you are at war. Will you dare to defy enemy schemes? Will you dare to fight for the things that matter? Will you dare to become a man of God? Cartoons, personal stories, deep questions, practical how-to steps, and Scripture all point youth ages 12 and up to fix their eyes on Jesus and draw near to Him as they fight the good fight, listen to God's voice and make wise decisions through His guidance, so they can become more than conquerors through every tough situation life presents. A leader's guide is included, but this workbook can also be studied as a devotional in personal quiet times.

Christian Fantasy Adventure Novels with a Purpose

Rescue from the Kingdom of Darkness
Book 1: Chronicles of the Kingdom of Light

Snatched from their summer fun by a sudden tragedy, six friends loyal to the King of Light embark upon an unforgettable adventure into the Kingdom of Darkness to rescue a young boy held hostage by evil creatures. Astride such mystical mounts as a winged tiger, a flying unicorn, and a giant cobra, these ordinary young people engage in an extraordinary battle that will cost them more than they counted on. As they struggle against monsters—and even each other—to overcome the fight against night, the friends soon discover the true enemy that must be conquered is the enemy within themselves. Readers will enjoy a fun read while learning to listen to God's voice, walk in truth rather than lies, find freedom from fear, and fight the good fight. Based on bedtime stories created by Vincent to help her children live who they are in Christ, this first book in the *Chronicles of the Kingdom of Light* is an inspirational allegory for young people filled with adventure, humor, and some truths that just might change their lives.

Sands of Surrender
Book 2: Chronicles of the Kingdom of Light

Banished by the King of Light, Cory cannot continue the search for his kidnapped brother until he discovers a way back into the Kingdom of Darkness where the boy is held prisoner. When creatures of Darkness offer to lead him there, he agrees to follow, a decision that costs him his freedom and exposes a plot against his family so dangerous he may not make it out alive. Meanwhile, Victoria sets out on her own misadventure to rescue her friend, but her decisions place those she loves in such terrible peril, Cory's life is not the only one she must save. Vincent uses humor and adventure to present truths that open the door to freedom from strongholds and generational curses, and walking in intimacy with the King of Kings.

Pure-As-Gold Children's Books

by Mikaela Vincent

MoreThanAConquerorBooks.com

Equipping young hearts today for the battles of tomorrow.

Out You Go, Fear!

Is your child afraid of the night? Does he sometimes "see" monsters in the dark? Does she have nightmares or awake in a panic? Do you? This story about a fearful, but eventually brave boy addresses night fears most children experience. Through colorful pictures, sound truths, and a fun storyline, Vincent offers children ages 4-8 (and parents too!) steps to freedom from fear so they can sleep in peace. Includes tips for parents on helping their children to freedom from nightmares and the effects of traumatic memories.

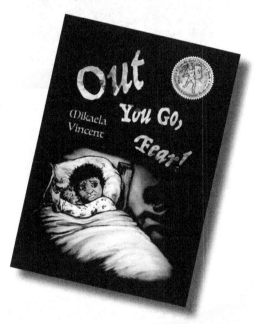

I Want a Horse!

Have you ever wanted something so much it was all you could think of or dream about? In this inspirational picture book for ages 4-8, Mikaela Vincent uses colorful artwork, imaginative poetry and heartwarming humor to tell the story of a young girl who asks for her heart's desire only to discover a treasure she already has that surpasses her imaginations. Moms and daughters will especially enjoy a deep bond reading together this fun interchange between an ambitious little girl and her wise and creative mother.

I Want to See Jesus!

This easy-to-read book for ages 3-7 uses colorful drawings and simple words to teach just-beginning readers that Jesus is always with us, even when we can't see Him.

Made in the USA
Columbia, SC
13 July 2020